MW00474529

ST SYMEON THE NEW THEOLOGIAN
ON THE MYSTICAL LIFE
vol. 2: On Virtue and Christian Life

St Symeon the New Theologian
ON THE MYSTICAL LIFE: THE ETHICAL DISCOURSES

vol. 1: *The Church and the Last Things*
    (ISBN 0-88141-142-6)

vol. 2 *On Virtue and Christian Life*
    (ISBN 0-88141-143-4)

vol. 3: *Life, Times and Theology*
    (ISBN 0-88141-144-2)

St Symeon the New Theologian

ON THE MYSTICAL LIFE: THE ETHICAL DISCOURSES
Vol. 2: On Virtue and Christian Life

Translated from the Greek and introduced

by

ALEXANDER GOLITZIN

ST. VLADIMIR'S SEMINARY PRESS
CRESTWOOD, NY 10707-1699
1996

The benefactors who have made this publication possible wish to dedicate it in thanksgiving for their children, Michael, David, King and Olivia.

Library of Congress Cataloging-in-Publication Data

Symeon the New Theologian, Saint, 949-1022
    On the mystical life: the ethical discourses / St. Symeon the New Theologian; translated from the Greek and introduced by Alexander Golitzin.
        p.   cm.
    Includes bibliographical references and indexes.
    ISBN 0-88141-142-6 (vol. 1)
    ISBN 0-88141-143-4 (vol. 2)
    Contents: vol. 2 (alk. paper)
    1. Spiritual life—Orthodox Eastern Church—Early works to 1800. 2. Monastic and religious life—Early works to 1800. 3. Mysticism—Orthodox Eastern Church—Early works to 1800. 4. Orthodox Eastern Church—Doctrines—Early works to 1800. I. Golitzin, Alexander. II. Title.
BX382.S96   1995
248.4'819—dc20   95-36925
                                                                CIP

Translation © 1996
St. Vladimir's Seminary Press

ISBN 0–88141–143–4

PRINTED IN THE UNITED STATES OF AMERICA

Contents

PREFACE

The present volume continues and completes the translation of the *Ethical Discourses* of St. Symeon the New Theologian (949-1022), sometime abbot of the Monastery of St. Mamas in Constantinople, and perhaps the most remarkable and influential mystic to appear in the history of the medieval Byzantine Church. As the introduction to Symeon's thought in volume III, forthcoming, will seek to demonstrate, the New Theologian's mysticism was consciously and thoroughly in harmony with the doctrinal, liturgical, and ascetical traditions of Eastern Christianity. What made him unique in virtually all the literature of the Christian East was the open and emphatic appeal to his own, personal experience. He was the first and, so far as one can tell, the last in the long history of Byzantium to insist on the use of the first person singular—"I"—in order to affirm the ancient emphasis of the Eastern Church on the aim of the Gospel as "deification," *theosis*: "God became as we are in order to make us even as He is Himself," according to the formula of St. Irenaeus of Lyons at the close of the second century. St. Symeon not only agreed, but added that he had himself experienced this truth, and indeed had seen with his own eyes the light of divinity given him by the grace of the Holy Spirit in Christ. That deification should be affirmed was altogether unexceptional, but to declare as Symeon did that one had oneself been the object of divine visitation broke sharply with traditional reticence and, most especially, with the conservative character of the Byzantine religious establishment. The New Theologian was as a result the subject of controversy throughout his active life.

Controversy is thus very much the fore in the pages that follow. Volume I of this series, including *Discourses* I-III, X and XIV, sets the boundaries of St. Symeon's reply to his critics by concentrating on certain accepted givens, notably the Church as the body of the risen Christ (I-II and XIV), the sacraments as the communication of this new reality (III), and thus the possibility in the present life of consciously perceiving the light of the world to come (X). In this, the second volume, Symeon expands his argument against the background of the traditional language of Eastern Christian asceticism. He is also throughout defending not only his own experience, but as well the authority of his spiritual father, Symeon the Elder or "the Pious" (d. ca. 986). Thus the virtue of dispassion, *apatheia,* provides the subject of *Discourses* IV and VI, wherein the New Theologian vigorously asserts the real possibility of liberation from sinful desires and points to the elder Symeon as an example. In *Discourses* VII and XI he addresses, respectively, the proper role of the tools of asceticism—i.e., fasting, vigils, poverty, etc.—and the true meaning of conformity to the Cross of Christ through struggle with the passions. The latter concludes with a thunderous warning against any who dare to take up the charge of the pastorate without having acquired the presence of God beforehand. Discourse V takes issue with "those who say that they have the Holy Spirit within themselves, but not consciously." St. Symeon replies that, to the contrary, the very substance of Christianity is the conscious perception of the divine presence and, in *Discourse* IX, he dwells on the character of those who perceive this presence, how they are to be discerned, and points again to his spiritual father as a shining example, as well as to the inner darkness of those who venture, out of ignorance, to speak ill of him.

The four remaining and shorter discourses are quite different in their tone, if not in the burden of their message. There is no hint of controversy. Rather, these brief talks breathe instead the sort of atmosphere that one might expect of an abbot preaching to his monks in the quiet of a well-ordered monastery. *Discourse* VIII takes up faith and love, and in the process makes typically striking use of two ancient images in Christian tradition, the "pearl" of divine presence and "pregnancy" with the Holy Spirit. *Discourses* XII and XIII are spiritual interpretations of, respectively, Ephesians 5:16 and I Corinthians 15:47, while *Discourse* XV expands on the venerable term for ascetic withdrawal, *hesychia*, meaning literally "quiet," but traditionally denoting the life of an anchorite or recluse. In the last discourse particularly, St. Symeon anticipates certain of these themes and central biblical texts of the fourteenth century movement, known as "hesychasm," which would play an enormously influential role in the life—both then and thereafter—of the Orthodox Church. Thanks, indeed, to those fourteenth and fifteenth century monks, as well as later on in the eighteenth and nineteenth centuries to such as St. Nicodemus of the Holy Mountain and St. Theophan the Recluse, the memory of the New Theologian was renewed and his writings preserved for the present day.

On the scriptural citations and other matters: citations are taken and numbered from the Revised Standard Version, save in those cases where St. Symeon is either conflating or quoting loosely from the text, or else where his version of—in particular—the Psalms does not correspond with the Masoretic base of the RSV. In former cases the bracketed reference will be preceded by "cf.," and in the latter it will be accompanied by the letters LXX. The titles of the discourses in boldface are abbreviated versions of the originals supplied by, probably, Symeon's disciple and original editor, Nicetas Stethatos. The subtitles in italics have been added by the present editor for the reader's convenience.

FOURTH ETHICAL DISCOURSE

Introduction

Discourse IV is devoted to the summit of the virtues, dispassion (*apatheia*), as the necessary prerequisite for the vision of God. Opening with a shot across the bows of his adversaries, Symeon states that only those who are themselves free of the passions can speak of dispassion. Such freedom is indeed possible, unfolding within the Christian by degrees until he or she discovers that it is the power of God Himself at work within the heart and so arrives, longing fulfilled, at the vision of "the single light of divinity." Again we find the theme of the spiritual senses, but this time more fully developed than in the preceding discourse and worked out in terms chiefly of two metaphors, the analogy of the soul with the Trinity which we saw in *Discourse* III, and what Symeon refers to as the "full measure of the mature man in Christ," borrowing from Ephesians 4:13. In the latter metaphor the members of the human body are portrayed as corresponding to the different virtues. Chief of the virtues and head of the body is love, that agency through which the body receives life and power, and "this love," Symeon declares, "is Christ God" Himself. Here is the true wealth which the Father offers His children in the Holy Spirit, and here is the fulfillment of every human desire and longing. The New Theologian concludes by testifying openly to his own, personal knowledge of the "blessed passion," and his "experience in perception and vision" of union with God.

ON THE GRACES AND GIFTS DISCLOSED WITHIN
DISPASSION (APATHEIA)[1]

*To speak of dispassion requires dispassion: Symeon's
claims versus false "authorities"*

Just as the man who wishes to gaze directly at the sun's
brilliance is obliged to cleanse the eyes of his body, so, too, is
he who sets out to discuss dispassion required to have the pupils
of his soul, I mean the senses, free from every evil lust and
impassioned thought. Otherwise, he will be troubled in his
mind and be unable to look directly at the heights of its purity
and at its depths, and will not worthily comprehend the multitude and grandeur of its activities and gifts, nor be able to
articulate them clearly. If, indeed, he were to consider the
principles of dispassion while troubled in mind and with an
impure heart, he would, as incapable of freely explaining its
activities, likely fall from even those partial benefits which he
had received from it. He would, in fact, reduce it to nothing by,
as it were, dishonoring and obscuring its glory. So is it written:

> To everyone who has will more be given, and he will
> have abundance; but from him who has not, even what
> he has will be taken away [Mt 25:29].

Obviously, therefore, as many as possess dispassion love it
and are loved exceedingly by it. They talk about it without
tiring, are on fire with longing for it, and so are rendered by it
still more dispassionate. As many, however, as are still bound
even by the least passing lust for the world and the latter's
things, or to some passion of the body or soul, are far away
from its haven. If, then, such people begin to talk about dispassion and attempt to lift up their minds to its heights, they are

1   For a definition of *apatheia*, see our *Introduction,* Part II, in
    vol. III, forthcoming.

instead dragged down like slaves and ensnared by lust for the passion to which they are bound. They are thus deprived of even that tranquillity of thought which they had earlier thought they possessed. This is altogether natural, "For," the Apostle says, "whatever overcomes a man, to that he is enslaved" [II Pet 2:19]. Filled with darkness as a result, they do not attribute the blame for what has happened to themselves, but have the temerity instead to confer this weakness upon all-powerful dispassion. This occurs because, while they have in no way acquired any experience of its spiritual perception and contemplation, nor of its all-efficacious activity, they use conjecture and varied and different speculations to figure out its qualities. Puffed up with so-called knowledge, they both love to talk about these matters, in this way and in that way, and so, confidently, to pontificate on subjects they know nothing about. As result, they not only cannot be persuaded to recognize and openly confess that weakness which, out of faithlessness and prejudice and long habit, has grown up and attached itself to them, but they also solemnly protest that all other men are like themselves, enslaved to the same passions. In effect, out of conceit and envy, they do not allow for the admission that anyone could ever be greater in virtue and temperance than themselves.

God forbid, however, that we, who are wretched and unworthy of speaking about such things, should pretend in such a way, falsifying the truth and carrying-on by talking confidently about matters whose activity we have not known first of all in ourselves by experience and not by words. What, though, we have been reckoned worthy of understanding and learning from those whose intellect was illumined by blessed dispassion, and what—I speak as one insane—we have heard spoken mystically in our ear by the same dispassion, that we shall proclaim from the roof-tops, in accordance with the grace which commands us from above, and in order that we not be condemned like the servant who hid his talent. Thus, just as you have heard the Master say: "Many are called, but few are chosen" [Mt 22:14], and "In My Father's house are many rooms" [Jn 14:2], just so do I want all of you to know that, while there are many who are holy, there are few who are dispassionate. Furthermore, among the latter there are great differences. Pay close attention now to the exact sense of what I have to say.

Degrees of dispassion and of other virtues: our capacities and God's grace

Dispassion of the soul is one thing and dispassion of the body another. While the former indeed sanctifies the body, the latter, in and of itself, profits its possessor not a bit. One thing is the immobility of the body's members and even the soul's passions, quite another the possession of virtue. While the former derives from nature, the latter has the habit of suppressing all the natural motions. It is one thing not to lust for any of the world's luxuries and pleasures, and quite another to long for the eternal good things of heaven. Many, each for his own reason, have held the former in contempt, but there are altogether few who have given thought to the second. Thus, while it is one thing not to seek out that glory which is of men, it is another to depend on God's glory and seek it without fail. Many have rejected the first, although dominated by other passions. Exceedingly few have been reckoned worthy, after much effort and pain, of laying hold on the second. While it is one thing to be satisfied with cheap clothing and not to desire splendid robes, it is something else again to be clothed with God's own light. For many have despised the first while at the same time being dragged down by ten thousand other lusts, but it is only those who have been arrayed in the second who have been made worthy of becoming sons of the light and of the day.

It is one thing to speak humbly, another to think humbly, and humility is one thing while the blossom of humility is another, and yet another the latter's fruit and the beauty of that fruit, and still another the energies which come out from the last. Of these, some are proper to us, and some are not. It is our part to conceive, think, reason, say, and do everything which brings us toward humility. Holy humility, though, and the rest of its characteristics, its charismata together with its energies, are God's own gift. They do not belong to that which is ours [by nature], so that we may take no pride in them. No one, however, will ever chance to be made worthy of these gifts unless first, like laying down seeds for them, he does everything which is his to do.

It is one thing neither to be stung nor angered by affronts and insults, nor by temptations and trials, and another to be pleased by them. It is one thing to pray for the people who do such things, and another to love them with all one's soul as benefactors, and still another to impress on one's spirit the face of each one of them, and then, with tears of sincere love, to embrace them dispassionately as true friends without the least trace of dislike making its nest in the soul. Greater, however, even than the last of which I spoke is it when someone in the midst of trials maintains an attitude of sameness and equilibrium with respect both to those who revile and slander him to his face, and to all the others who judge, or insult, or condemn him, or who spit in his face; and indeed, who remains so even with respect to those who bear themselves outwardly with an appearance of friendliness, but who, behind his back, practise the same things against him as the others, even though he is aware of this, too. I am also of the opinion that there is a stage yet incomparably higher than the last: to have arrived at complete forgetfulness of whatever it is one may have suffered and never to recall it, whether those who have done the injury are present or not, and, in addition, to behave toward these people, whether in conversation or at table, as toward friends, without having any second thoughts. These are all the works of men who walk in the light. As many, however, as learn that they are far away from such men and such behavior, let them neither be deluded nor fool themselves, but let them rather know of a certainty that they walk in darkness.

In addition to the above, it is one thing to fear God, and another to do His commandments. As it is written: "O fear the Lord, you His saints" [Ps 34:9], and again: "Depart from evil, and do good" [Ps 37:27]. Inactivity is one thing, quiet [*hesychia*] another, and still another is silence. Again, retreat [*anachoresis*] is one thing, moving from place to place another, and perfect exile [*xeniteia*] yet another. Not sinning is one thing, and the practise of the commandments another. Still more, it is one thing to oppose and do battle with one's enemies, and another to vanquish them completely, to subdue and put them to death. While the former is proper to fighters and to saints, provided they arrive at being perfected in it, the second belongs to the dispassionate and perfect who have clearly, through much labor and sweat, triumphed over their enemies, have gained complete victory over them, and have been vested in splendor with the life-bearing mortification of Christ.

Progress towards dispassion comes in answer to prayer

Thus while many, each for his own reasons, have certainly dedicated themselves to these things, there are exceedingly few who do so with an innate fear and love for God, and with unwavering faith. The latter, indeed, alone, aided by grace, rapidly achieve the practise of virtue, and, making progress with respect to all that we have outlined, press forward hour by hour. As for the others, according to Scripture they are "left to wander in trackless wastes" [Ps 107:40]. It is also written concerning them:

> I gave them over to their stubborn hearts, to follow their
> own counsel [Ps 81:12]; And since they did not see fit
> to acknowledge God, God gave them up to a base mind
> and to improper conduct [Rom 1:28].

Therefore, those who have laid down a good foundation of faith
and hope, with fear and trembling, on the rock of obedience to
their spiritual fathers, and who build without second thoughts
upon this foundation of submission, and receive what is commanded them by their fathers as if it came from the mouth of
God, immediately succeed in denying themselves. For, to fulfill
not one's own will, but that of one's spiritual father for the sake
of God's commandments and of exercise in virtue, accomplishes not only the denial of oneself, but as well complete
mortification with respect to the world.

Thus as in a desert, or better, as outside the world, such a
person arrives at perfect perception, and, seized by ineffable
fear and trembling, cries out to God with all his soul—like
Jonah from the whale, like Daniel from the lions' den, like the
three youths from the fiery furnace, like Manasses from the
statue of bronze. And the all-good Master Who lays down His
life for us sinners, on hearing the anguished groans of his cry
of petition, straightway delivers him, as from the whale, out of
the deeps of ignorance and the gloom of love for the world,
such that he never goes back to it even in thought. He delivers
him from the lions' den, which is to say, from the evil lusts
which seize and devour the souls of men; from the fiery
furnace, as from those passionate predispositions which possess all men, which burn and ravage like fire, dragging us down
by force to shameful deeds and kindling in us the flame of the
passions. The Master bedews him with the Holy Spirit, and
renders him proof against that fire. He delivers him from the
statue of bronze, as from this earthly, heavy, and impassioned
flesh of ours in which our soul dwells and is dreadfully held

prisoner. Shackled and weighed down by the flesh, it abides motionless and unready in all respects with regard to every virtue, and to the doing of God's commandments. When it is set free—although not separated—from the body, it cries out with the prophet David and says: "You have loosed my sackcloth and girded me with gladness, that my soul may praise You" [Ps 30:11-12]. Nor this alone, but, together with the Apostle Paul, it also gives thanks and says:

> Thanks be to God through Jesus Christ our Lord. . . . For the law of the Spirit of life in Christ Jesus has set me free from the law of sin and death [Rom 7:25 and 8:2].

When thus, by the grace of Christ, these things have been accomplished, when, to repeat myself, one has been delivered from the ignorance and gloom of love for the world, and has been released from evil and shameful lusts, and has been set free from him who holds us captive under the law of sin—what then is this man going to do? Will he then use this freedom to become carefree and comfortable? What a thought! Such are properly the thoughts of slaves, not of free men. For he who has been deemed worthy of this freedom knows that he has been set free of the law of sin in order that he never again be thus enslaved, but instead, that he become enslaved to the righteousness of Him Who both is and is entitled the Sun of righteousness, Christ our God. And, that I may give you an illustration of the sort of good disposition which this man will henceforth show toward God, let me take my example from the sorts of things that often occur among human beings.

God is like a gracious Emperor

It is as if a compassionate and humane emperor were to see one of his servants voluntarily taken captive and enslaved by a certain tyrant, then vexed with clay and brick and mud, suffering pitiably, and forced to serve the unclean lusts of that same tyrant. The emperor then comes and snatches his servant out of that ugly and vile service, shows him to be a free man, and, leading him back to the palace, restores him without blaming or reproaching him in any way. Now, that servant, as one delivered from such great miseries, will in his love for his master be ambitious to show himself the more zealous with regard to the latter's commandments, in order—since he remembers continually from what great evils he was delivered—to demonstrate his great and ardent love for the one who saved him. Imagine with me that it is just so with the man who has enjoyed God's succour. And, just as that emperor, on seeing the servant fulfilling his will eagerly and with all humility, even if his service is not required (for the king has an innumerable multitude of servitors) but rather because of his gratitude, will in turn give the servant further proof of his immeasurable love for him; just so you may take it to be the case with God. For neither will he who has enjoyed the freedom of God's Spirit ever cease from doing His will with ever-increasing ardor, nor will the eternal King and God, so long as He sees the man extending himself daily in His service, deprive him of the good things of everlasting life by not lavishing these things on him freely. Of those benefits and good things which God does for his servants there is neither measure nor comprehension; and He bestows some on them now, and others He will grant them later.

God's gift is Himself: Food, and drink, and light[2]

We would certainly like to name for your Charity a few of those benefits which the merciful God gives to those in this life. Some of them are mentioned in holy Scripture. Others are known from experience itself. Since men display every zeal

2 We have no idea who the person is whom Symeon refers to here as "your charity," but it is quite possible that this personage is not a real individual, but a kind of all-purpose interlocutor, a literary device.

and concern for the following three things, I mean for wealth, honor, and glory, together with the freedom and joy and enjoyment which these procure for us, these are first of all what our Master and God richly bestows on those who cast all aside, take up the cross, and follow in His footsteps without turning back. Instead of corruptible wealth, He gives them His entire Self. Do you understand the power of this saying? Do you comprehend its dreadful wonder? Just as the wealthy of this world squander their money on whatever needs and lusts and enjoyments they may wish, so, too, our good Master gives Himself to His true servants and fills their every desire and longing, as much as they want and beyond, and fills them with every good thing, keeping nothing back, and generously provides them unceasingly with incorruptible and everlasting delight.

And first of all they are filled with ineffable joy, because it is not the world or anything in the world which they have acquired, but the Maker of all things, and Lord, and Master. Then they are clothed with the light, with Christ God Himself, wholly, throughout their entire bodies. They see themselves adorned with ineffable glory, with a divine robe of lightning splendor. They hide their gaze, unable to bear the vision of their vesture's incomprehensible and unendurable luster, to such a point that they look for a place to hide in order to go there and be delivered from the great weight of their glory. Then the same Master becomes for them food and drink, everlasting and undying. To some, as many as are still infants in Christ and are not yet ready to partake of strong meat, He appears as a breast of light, placed in the mouth of their intellect to suckle them. For others He becomes at once food and drink, introducing them to such great sweetness that they want never—or, better, can never—separate themselves from Him. For those who have been weaned, He offers Himself as a loving Father, correcting and educating His children.

The loving Father

Just as a father who loves his children makes his sons dine with him but, when he sees they are conducting themselves carelessly with regard to their lessons and distracting themselves with unprofitable matters, expels them from his table and orders his servants not to give them any food, in order to teach them not to be scornful and careless, so does our good Master and God dispose Himself for the sake of those who are His servants and, by virtue of His grace and love for mankind, His sons. He gives them Himself, "the bread which comes down from heaven and gives life to the world" [Jn 6:33], and they are nourished continually to satiety from Him and with Him, and through participation are transformed into life everlasting, and are sanctified in body and soul. But, when they neglect the commandments and, by free exercise of their will, conduct themselves scornfully or slothfully, and busy themselves with some worldly affair, inclining thus toward what is unsuitable and not proper to piety, then the Nourisher of all deprives them of Himself. Then, when they have come to an awareness of that good of which they have been deprived, and have turned around immediately and sought it out continually, and, not having found it, beat their breasts, weep, and mourn for themselves, and lay on themselves every kind of suffering, and long for every sort of distress, and trial, and dishonor, in order that their loving Father might see their sorrows and their voluntary woe, and, taking pity on them, turn about and give Himself to them once again. Which, indeed, He does. So they are restored to their former condition and glory, with yet greater assurance, and to the same delight in the good things "which eye has not seen, nor ear heard, nor the heart of man conceived" [I Cor 2:9]. They revere their Father more than before, and tremble before Him as Master, lest through inattentiveness they be implicated in the same evils as before and so be cast away from Him.

All wealth save God's is scrap and carrion

Those who repent vigorously do these things and practise them, and so they attain to the good things described. On the other hand, as many as grow weary of the labors and sorrows and difficulties of repentance, and give themselves over to laziness and comfort, like unworthy and bastard children, and moreover as contemptuous, and who prefer the pleasures of the body to the eternal goods and to God Himself, such are no longer deemed worthy of this delight, nor indeed of the vesture of divine glory, but justly deprive themselves of the wealth of God's goodness and become like dogs without a master. For just as masterless dogs wander around the squares and alleys of the city looking to snatch a bone somewhere or a cast-off piece of old leather, or even lick up the blood and dung of slaughtered cattle, and, if they should chance on some carrion, they eat insatiably, leaving the cadaver none the earlier but rather fighting among themselves to chase away the other dogs until they have stripped the bones not only of the entrails, but of the very last shreds of tissue; just so, too, are those [monks] who run about the doors of rich and poor like mountebanks in order to pocket some contribution of gold or silver or copper, because they have fallen away from the true wealth which passes not away. And, when they have gotten their way, then they rest for a bit, as if they were satiated and in need of nothing more. When again, as a consequence of despair, the famine of insatiate desire seizes them, then they give themselves up immediately to their begging as before. They are wretched with respect to the present age—even if they should possess all the wealth in the world—and even more wretched with regard to the future one, because they have voluntarily expelled themselves from everlasting life.

To deprive them of any excuse, God in fact has revealed to them the riches of His grace, and has honored them with a taste of heavenly gifts and made them partakers of the Holy Spirit. Yet, as the divine Paul cries out, "They did not honor Him as God", or love Him, or receive His infinite goodness,

> ...or give thanks to Him, but they became futile in their thinking, and their senseless minds were darkened. Claiming to be wise, they became fools [Rom 1:21-22].

However, this is not the way of it among those who fear the Lord. Rather, as many as have endured the corrections of their own Father and Master, like grateful servants and legitimate sons, say: "I will bear the Lord's punishment because I have sinned before Him," and, in another key: "The sufferings of this present time are not worth comparing with the glory that is to be revealed to us" [Rom 8:18]. Thus, as we said, they abide in their daily correction and constant penitence, not shying away from it or becoming annoyed by it, but, disciplined in the manner we have described, they abide forever in the Father's house, radiantly clothed, eating at their Father's table, beholding His glory and the wealth which they will come to inherit. When they have grown up, have been disciplined, and have attained to the measure of the stature of the perfect man, then the good Father gives all that is His into their hands.

The virtues and the image of the Trinity: the complete man in Christ

Let us now first of all define what is the measure of spiritual maturity and the height of Christ's fulness, and then we shall proceed to what belongs to the Father, and to how He gives it into the hands of those who believe in Him. So, pay careful attention to the meaning of what we shall have to say.

The measure of the stature of the fulness of Christ [Eph 4:13] is the following, considered spiritually. Beginning with the foundation, its feet are faith and holy humility, a firm ground and unshaken. Its legs and ankles and calves and knees and thighs are non-possession, nakedness, voluntary exile, willing submission for the sake of Christ, obedience, and eager service. The members and parts which one is obliged to hide are unceasing prayer of the mind, the sweetness which derives from the shedding of tears, the joy of the heart and its inexpressible consolation. Kidneys and hips are the standing and endurance at prayer and at worship services, and that which derives from them, the kindling of one's appetite for the contemplation of God and union with Him, such as the divine David describes when he says: "Set on fire my reins and my heart" [Ps 25:2, LXX]; and Paul: "Stand therefore, having girded your loins with truth" [Eph 6:14]; and Peter, the leader of the Apostles:

> Therefore gird up your minds, be sober, set hopes fully upon the grace that is coming to you at the revelation of Jesus Christ as children of obedience [I Pet 1:13-14].

"Grace" is what he calls the gift of the all-Holy Spirit which makes us co-participants and communicants of God.

The belly, stomach, and apparatus of the intestines are the soul's intellectual workshop and capacity for reception, within which you should conceive the rational faculty as the heart in the middle, and, together with the rational faculty, the faculties of irritation and appetite. Like the sides, nerves, muscles and fat, there are meekness, simplicity, forebearance, compassion, and reverence to hold together and bind up, envelope and conceal, and not suffer one to look away to visible things nor lust after anything out there. Neither do they allow room for the remembrance of wrongs, nor envy, nor jealousy, nor wrath, nor permit that these passions should ever be seen. The passionate inclinations are never directed to what is exterior, but are kept hidden. In as much as these inclinations are kept within and are securely guarded by the virtues which we have listed, the reasonable faculty can distinguish and separate the worse from the better, and indicate to the appetite which things it ought relatively to attach itself to, which it should love, and which it must turn away from and hate. The irritable faculty is situated between these two like a kind of prudent servant, carrying out their decisions and co-operating with their wishes, and raising resolution up to manliness and assistance in the action of good men and of bad, whichever case applies.

Since the God Who has fashioned them is incomparably greater than everything visible, he who has been honored with reason and has kept his intellect untroubled and unconfused by impassioned predispositions, will, as we have said, naturally prefer and love the Master and Maker of all things instead of and prior to all else. Toward Him alone will he lift up all his faculty of appetite, giving it to understand, as it were, and saying to it: "Listen to me, and look! Touch with dread, taste the undefiled sweetness, smell the fragrant oil [*myron*] of the Spirit, and know that no one is more beautiful than He, nor more delightful, nor sweeter, nor, in sum, more powerful or more glorious, nor indeed more able to make you alive, and incorruptible and immortal." When, therefore, appetite is fulfilled by all these good things, then the whole of the irritable faculty is as well wholly mingled with both the appetitive and rational faculties, and the three are one in the contemplation of the Threefold Unity, and enter into the joy itself of their Master. At that point their threefold distinction is no longer discernible, but they are wholly one. Whenever thus these powers, in the simplicity which is uniquely of the One and Good, turn towards what is here-below, to the discernment of good from evil, at that very moment their volition and choice, and their turning away from what is contrary to the divine will is shown to be indivisible, for in such instances the activity of the irritable faculty is alone operative.[3]

3   Here again we find the psychological image of the Trinity, this

We have still more and other things to say about these matters, about stomach and liver, about food and drink, hunger and thirst, but, in order not to over-extend our discourse and betray what should not be betrayed to those hunters of words who are used to enriching themselves with foreign goods, we have left these veiled in silence for those who choose to seek them out through the knowledge of experience. Let us instead return to the subject at hand. Since we have built the body of the stature which is Christ's up to the belly and shoulders, we are obliged to continue up to the head in order to complete it spiritually as whole and sound.

Thus we must add chest and back, shoulders, arms, hands, and a neck to this body of spiritual maturity. As the body's chest you should imagine compassion, by which the breasts of love for mankind unreservedly pour out the milk of alms for orphans, widows, and all others, as was said by the saint: "Brothers, lay hold on the bowels of compassion." I will leave you to find out whence this milk is supplied to the breasts, and how it operates. The back means the willing taking on oneself of others' burdens, and carrying about in oneself the wounds of the Lord Jesus, as the Apostle says: "You, the strong, bear the burdens of the weak" [Rom 15:1]; and again: "Henceforth let no man trouble me, for I bear on my body the marks of the Lord Jesus" [Gal 6:17]; and the Lord's own words through the prophet: "I gave my back to the smiters, and cheeks to slap-

time tied to the traditional division of the soul's faculties into appetite (*epithymia*), irritability (*thymos*), and reason (*nous, to logistikon*). So far as we know, this passage is unique not only to Symeon, but to the whole Greek Christian tradition. The New Theologian does not, however, identify any of the three faculties with one or another of the Persons of the Trinity. His idea is rather that the unity of the soul's three powers working together mirrors the single life and being of the divine Triad. Once more, see our *Introduction,* Part II, in vol. III, forthcoming.

ping" [Is 50:6]. Even if no occasion for suffering these things should arise, we must still expect and prepare ourselves for them hourly. Shoulders and arms are the capacity for patience and endurance in temptations and afflictions, through and with which the hands are enabled to act. And I call hands the readiness and zeal for every obedience and for the doing of God's commandments, which, without much patience and endurance, no one can ever attain. In addition to the above, this maturity in Christ also has spiritual hands, by which it consoles those of little faith, raises up the fallen, and binds up the wounded, pouring oil and wine on their wounds which, together with many other activities in word and deed, it does every day for its neighbors, by which it touches the hem of the Master, and offers bread to its Lord, and puts the cup in His hands. Thus is it that, with every breath, we feed Him Who feeds us with the food which He said we must desire and long for. And blessed is he who knows these things, and has them, and offers them to his Master, because He Who is borne aloft by the cherubim will make that man recline in the Kingdom of Heaven and, according to His own promise which is no lie, will gird Himself and minister to him. Finally, the neck of this body is unwavering hope.

Love is the "head" of "the body of the virtues"

Now, by God's help and His grace, we have finished the whole body of a perfect man as I understand it to be, one complete in all its members. Only the head is still missing. But perhaps you thought we had said everything and not left out anything at all, as if everything were sufficient in what has been said for the completion of virtue and the soul's salvation? It is not so, not at all. For, just as the body which has all its members, yet is lacking its head, is quite dead and inactive, and again, as the head without all the rest of its body is of itself just a head and unable to manifest its proper activities while still

separated from the body, just so should you consider it to be
with regard to the spiritual body which is fashioned by us in
co-operation with the Holy Spirit. Everything we have described is useless and stale without its head, even if many
people are foolishly inclined to think they have achieved the
whole by their partial accomplishment and possession of the
virtues. Being dead, they have no perception of the good which
they lack. Although we have recounted the virtues severally in
order to provide a clear example and knowledge, yet without
the head and the natural conjunction of all the members with
each other, it is impossible for these qualities to cohere and be
strong. Just as it is impossible for the body of a little child to
grow up when deprived of its head but, when both are joined
and receive their nourishment from one another—the body
through the mouth and head in its turn by the blood which is
pumped up to it from the body—the whole man is nourished
and grows. You must understand with me and see that is the
same regarding the head and its addition to the spiritual body.
Now, in order to make this more clear for you, listen well while
I summarize what has been said.

Thus you have the foundations of the virtues, faith and
humility, and upon these two all the virtues I have described
are built up and comprise the whole body, completed right up
to its neck, which is hope. While the latter is raised up above
the rest of the body, by itself alone, unconnected with the head,
it dies together with the other members of the body. It has no
place from which it may receive the breath and respiration of
the Spirit Who quickens and moves the body and its members,
nor any way to partake at all of the immortal food. For this
reason, in order not to leave the measure of the full stature of
Christ incomplete, we add to it holy love, its true head. We did
not imagine this by ourselves, nor contrive it. Not at all. Rather,
we have been taught by that same Holy Spirit which St. Paul

possessed who said: "So faith, hope, and love abide, these three; but the greatest of these is love" [I Cor 13:13]; and again:

> If I have all faith, so as to remove mountains, and if I have all knowledge and understand all mysteries, and if I give away all I have, and if I speak the tongues of men and of angels, and if I give my body to be burned, but have not love, I gain nothing [I Cor 13:1-3].

Therefore faith, with the mediation of hope, is invisibly and imperceptibly—I speak as still to infants—made zealous, is taught and enabled by holy love, and so accomplishes everything we have discussed. Faith accomplishes them all, and through them it feeds and ministers to the head and makes it grow, I mean holy love. The latter in turn, as ministered to and growing, provides strength in proportion to the remaining body of the virtues, and prepares them to stretch out still further toward that which is before [cf. Phil. 3:14].

"And this love...is Christ:" the robe of glory

Thus assembled and held together, kept in harmony by holy love, all the members of the spiritual body grow up little by little, bone to bone and joint to joint. And this love, the head of all the virtues, is Christ and God. For this reason He descended to earth and, becoming man, partook of our earthly flesh: in order that He might impart in turn of His essential divinity to us and, thus making us spiritual and completely incorruptible, lead us up to heaven. This is the love which the Apostle says has been richly poured out in our hearts, that is, the participation and sharing in His divinity by virtue of which we are made one with God. St. John the Theologian, on the same subject, also says: "Perfect love casts out fear" [I Jn 4:18]; and that "He who fears is not perfected in love" [I Jn 4:18]; and again: "See what love the Father has given us, that we should be called children of God" [I Jn 3:1]. Here he calls love the Holy Spirit, through Whom we also receive adoption to sonship.

No man can then see or receive this love, or be joined to it and possess it consciously as head, unless, as we said, he keeps his faith in Christ firm and unshakeable, and earnestly builds up upon this faith all the virtues discussed. Indeed, whoever has not seen nor been joined to it, nor partaken of its sweetness, cannot love it as it deserves, either. For how can someone love what he has not seen? "For he who does not love his brother", says the Apostle, "whom he has seen, cannot love God Whom he has not seen" [I Jn 4:20]. On the other hand, unless he loves Him first with all his soul, with all his heart, and with his natural intentions and everything which in our nature inclines us toward affection, he will not be made worthy of seeing Him. For, "He who loves Me," says the Lord, "will be loved by My Father;" and then He adds: "And I will love him and manifest Myself to him" [Jn 14:21]. This shows clearly that, unless someone loves God first of all with all his soul and proves his love for Him by denying both himself and the world, he is unworthy mystically of God's manifestation in the revelation of the Holy Spirit, nor does he possess Him as head, but is instead a dead body in spiritual works, is deprived of Christ, the life of all.

Those, however, who have been made worthy of being joined to and possessing Him as head—please! pay attention to my words!—become even themselves gods by adoption, become like the Son of God. O, what a wonder! For God the Father clothes them with the original vesture, the very mantle which the Lord wore before the foundation of the world. "For as many," says Paul, "of you as were baptized into Christ have put on Christ" [Gal 3:27]. Clearly, he means that it is the Holy Spirit Who alters them in a manner appropriate to God, an alteration which is strange, ineffable, and divine. David says concerning this: "This is the change of the right hand of the Most High" [Ps 77:10]; as also the disciple who rested on the

Lord's breast: "Behold, we are children now, but," he adds, "it does not yet appear"—obviously, for those who are in the world—"what we shall be. But we know"—that is, from the Spirit Whom He has given us—"that when He appears we shall be like Him" [I Jn 3:2]. And this is not all, but He also bestows on them the mind of Christ which shines above their heads, and which reveals mysteries to them which it is not lawful for a human tongue to utter [cf. II Cor. 12:14]. In addition, He gives them new eyes and new ears. And what are all the things I want to say? It is impossible to say them all. That entire world which is God Himself, with the Father and the Spirit, dwells in them. Each of them becomes a temple of God [cf. II Cor. 3:16 and 6:19] in perception and in knowledge, and at once cries aloud and says: "It is no longer I who live, but Christ Who lives in me" [Gal 2:20]; and again:

> When I was a child I spoke like a child, I thought like a child, I reasoned like a child; when I became a man, I gave up childish ways [I Cor 13:11].

It is on this account that I bear all things, endure all things, and bless when I am reviled, and pray when I am cursed, and endure when I am persecuted: "That the power of Christ may rest upon me" [II Cor 12:19].

The Cross: perfection is completed in suffering for Christ

This is therefore the stature of spiritual men, complete yet incomplete. Complete, I say, according to what is possible for us, but incomplete because its perfection in God is hidden away, and its fulness is death for the sake of Christ and His commandments. Thus, just as He completed the Law and gave Himself up for the whole world, endured the Cross and death while praying even for those who were crucifying Him: "Father, forgive them this sin; for they know not what they do" [Lk 23:34], so we ought, too, to carry about in ourselves the curse of death for His sake and for His commandments, for, indeed, the sake of our brothers' salvation, in order "to rely not on ourselves, but on God Who raises the dead" [II Cor 1:9]. And, if it should happen that we depart this life without a violent death, then the same shall be reckoned to us by our loving God as having occurred, in choice if not in deed, by virtue of our suffering and endurance, in accordance with the saying of the saint: "By my love for you, I die every day" [I Cor 15:31]. He does not say this because he has often in fact suffered death, but as having done so in intention, as he says again: "I press on to make it my own, because Christ Jesus has made me His own" [Phil 3:12]. So ought we always to pray for everyone who grieves or reviles us for whatever cause, and for all who are hostile toward us because of an evil disposition, and, indeed, for all the faithful and unfaithful, in order that we may attain to perfection and they be delivered from error and draw near the true faith.

No one could ever imagine these things by himself, or speak them, or receive them by hearing, let alone practise them in fact, unless the love of God had not first been poured out richly in his heart and he had thus obtained indwelling within him, the One Who said: "Apart from Me, you can do nothing" [Jn 15:5]. But, neither does one happen on this grace and gift unless he has first denied himself, as the Savior commanded and as we made clear above, and has zealously enslaved himself to the Lord and loved Him. Let no one deceive himself. Unless he has accepted this all irrevocably, let him know that he has neither been made worthy of the union with God which occurs through intelligible perception and knowledge and contemplation, nor will he ever be made worthy of it. For those who have merited the title of perfect men by virtue of sharing in God's grace, and have acquired spiritual stature in the measure described, these become wholly with God. They behold Him as much as they are themselves beheld by Him. God abides consciously in them, and they abide consciously in God, indivisibly and without separation.

When such men have well and truly arrived at this state of perfection, at that moment their heavenly Father places in their hands what is properly His own. By hands, you should understand certitude and assurance, while what belongs to Him are immortality, incorruptibility, the unmoving, unchanging, the eternal, impossible beauty of the glory which the Son had with the Father before the world was, as He Himself, the Word and Son of the Father, says: "Glorify Me, Father, with the glory which I had with You before the world was" [Jn 17:5]; and again: "The glory which You gave to Me I have given to them, that they may be one; as You, Father, are in Me, and I in them" [Jn 17:22]. From Him the light flows which is at once unapproachable for sinners, yet approachable for those in whom it rises like the dawn to become joy unspeakable, peace surpassing intellection, delight, enjoyment, and rejoicing in unsatiable surfeit now and for ages without end. And, to sum up, since I am unable to speak any more because I am myself stricken with amazement, the first-fruits of those good things, whose beauty no eye troubled by the passions can see, nor an ear stopped up with ignorance hear, which occur in no heart that is impure, which God has prepared for those who love Him [cf. I Cor. 2:9], these same first-fruits He Who is faithful and does not lie gives even here, already, to those who believe.

These, then, are those things proper to the Father which I promised beforehand to tell you of. And, as you have heard, He gives them to those who love Him and who live their lives on earth as if it were in heaven, who are in death as if they were already adorned with immortality, and who walk in the darkness as if it were day and light without evening. While still in this muddy body they breathe as in the paradise of delight, possessing in their midst the tree of life. Yes, indeed, they eat that which is the very food of the angels, the heavenly bread, whence all the immortal powers are nourished and quickened undefiled. Even while living in the midst of the world and its concerns, these blessed ones cry out in truth with Paul: "Our citizenship is in heaven" [Phil 3:20], there, where holy love makes its home, mingling with its lovers and shining richly about them, making them dispassionate and, in very truth, angels.

The false guides are like babies playing with the armor of warriors

Whoever, therefore, who, before having been joined and mingled wholly with love, calls himself dispassionate, or teaches others about it, or attempts to do the works of the dispassionate, or, on the contrary, refuses to believe in the works of the dispassionate, is like a tender infant who takes up the weapons of men before he is mature and promises to teach others about warfare. Nor does it stop there, but he also goes out and intrudes himself into the company of men and warriors and tries to accompany them to war. This is not only impossible, but comic as well, since he is encumbered all about by the weapons he is trying to carry. He is loaded down with them, tripped up by them, and is perhaps incapable of even getting up again. This is quite natural, since he does not know that those wounded in battle and taken off the field get up again and, having learned with experience, fight against their enemies more vigorously. So, if God commanded Moses not to send any who were cowardly out to war, how much more again must this apply to an infant, still incapable of walking or of dressing by himself, not to take up the stature of a man and attempt to do what is impossible for him.

Because, however:

We are not contending against flesh and blood, but against the principalities, against the powers, against

the world rulers of this present darkness, against the
spiritual hosts of wickedness in the heavenly places. . .
[Eph 6:12]

neither are our weapons fleshly and visible, but spiritual and
intelligible. This war is both invisible and is joined invisibly with
invisible enemies. It is therefore easy for any who think themselves special to present themselves to others as bold and courageous about these matters, and as supremely experienced in
the analysis and tactics of such warfare, indeed, as wise and
knowledgeable teachers of the art of conquest and victory over
the evil ones. Thus, by means of their empty talk and the delusion
of their syllogisms, they hurry to acquire the reputation of
single-handed warriors and victors over the enemy. While both
reproved and condemned by their own conscience as untried and
without experience in this warfare, they are unable to admit and
confess their weakness and inexperience since they are dominated by vainglory and the desire to impress others, and so are
terribly afraid of losing the good opinion of men.

Because their neighbors do not see them for what they are
in their soul, nor do others understand that they are naked of
the Spirit's weapons and are both weak and infantile, they hide
themselves under the fleece of hypocrisy and with sheep's
clothing. By means of their fine talk they want to appear to
everyone as people who have obtained through their efforts the
stature according to Christ. Yet they have not established their
foundations of faith and love firmly upon the rock, nor have
they raised up the edifice of the virtues upon Christ the foundation stone. On this account, being still hesitant and untested,
pushed around by every attack of temptations and the gusts of
evil thoughts, bound hand and foot, and thus tripping up, they
fall down pitiably. If they, who wear the mere form of piety
like a tent, were seen by others for what they really are, they
would neither be able to stand in the public eye, nor, I think,

would they want to be seen by anyone at all. Those indeed in particular who imagine they are superior to others in knowledge and reason, and who think they bear the imprint of royalty—and, in fact, who are honored and held in respect by most people as both learned and devout—differ in no way with respect to the invisible motions of their soul from those who are the most extravagant in malice.

An image of the saint: the moonlit sky

Come, though, all of you who want to be instructed about the glory of those men who are truly holy and dispassionate. Come, that is, you who desire it, who ardently long to possess it, and I will draw you a picture which shows the extent of their weaponry, and you will know their brilliance. Each of you, comparing himself with these saints, will know where he stands, and how far away all of us are from their courage, their worthiness and their power.

So then, picture with me the sky as it is on a clear and cloudless night. See, there is the moon's disk, full of limpid and purest light, and around it the halo which often appears. Now, with this in mind, turn your thought to what I am about to say. Each one of the saints, while yet in the body, is like that evening sky, and the heart of each like the moon's disk. Holy love is the all-efficacious and all-powerful light, far and incomparably greater than the light of our sun, which touches their hearts and, waxing in accordance with the capacity of each, fills them perfectly. Neither does it ever wane, like the light of the moon, but is always kept all light through the zeal and good works of the saints. And holy dispassion, like an aureole and a tabernacle, surrounds and cares for them, covers them wholly, and preserves them unwounded by any evil thought, let alone by sins, and sets them up as unhurt and free from all their foes. And, not only this, but it even renders them unapproachable for their enemies.

Do you see the glory which you truly desire? Do you

understand the grandeur of this image and how much each of us lacks the glory and brilliance of the saints? For this image is a type of what is actually being perfected in us—let it not be thought by our own efforts, God forbid!—but God established it beforehand and now brings it into being. In creating, the divine artisan and Word of God drew beforehand as on a tablet what would happen in the future for our salvation in order that, on seeing the type appear in perceptible things, we should not doubt that the real truth would be completed and perfected spiritually in our own inward being. Rather, knowing that each one of us is created by God as a second world, a great world in this small and visible one—as one of the theologians bears me witness[4]—we ought to want to appear in no wise worse than the unreasoning or soulless animals which the God Who loves mankind has created for our instruction, but instead be zealous for everything which is good in them while fleeing as much as we can the imitation of their defects.

Exhortation to struggle and long for the light of God

Dispensing with the rest, for there is much to say, I will bring just this to your attention and then conclude my discourse. Let everyone who is listening know that, just as we see day succeeding night, and night in turn coming from day, so we must believe and become convinced that we who are in the darkness of sin and spend our lives in it from birth are able, through faith and the practise of the commandments, to be led up to a divine day and a spiritual light, just as in turn, by sloth

4 Symeon is quoting Gregory of Nazianzus here (see ref. in *Introduction,* Part II, in vol. III, forthcoming). The idea is that the physical world, here the picture of the full moon on a cloudless night, is a God-intended image of the perfected human being. Elsewhere, and more often, Symeon applies the notion of microcosm reflecting macrocosm to the human soul and the Church. See again our *Introduction*, Part II, in vol. III).

and contempt and inattention, we fall into our former evils and
enter under the night of sin. In this respect if in nothing else we
must imitate our attendant and servant, the sun. For just as the
latter never stops shining and shedding light, but fulfills the
Master's command without ceasing, so should we, too, not will
to sit inattentively in the darkness of pleasure and the passions,
but instead keep the commandments of Him Who said: "Repent, for the Kingdom of God is at hand" [Mt 3:2]. Thus,
purified by virtue of daily and unceasing penitence, and by the
tears which spring from and through it, and by every other
good work, we must hasten as sons of the light to ascend to the
light which is above. So shall we also, possessing the sun of
righteousness shining within us, provide for our neighbors the
example of the immaterial day, the new earth and new heaven.
I mean, we shall not recount God's commandments by means
of vain and empty words, but by the works themselves, and so
become real and effective teachers in each and every way for
our less attentive brethren, and render them without excuse.

Therefore, let us not encourage our neighbors to laziness by
saying: "What is this then, and how is it possible for human
beings to achieve this?" and so make them even more reluctant
to practise the commandments. While I agree myself that many
things are impossible for the majority, I am saying this in
particular for those of my order [i.e., the monks] who are lazy
and do not choose to despise the world and reckon everything
in it as garbage; who are addicted to vainglory and lust after
wealth, and who take pleasure in the praises and honors which
are from men, and who thus also are under the wretched control
of vanity and conceit. For the present, I willingly overlook
those who wallow like pigs in the mud of sin's evils and carry
around the house of their soul empty of Him Who indwells the
faithful, Who cries daily to those who believe: "In the world
you have tribulation; but be of good cheer, I have overcome the

world" [Jn 16:33]. The former have sided with the enemy. As for the latter, however, who by faith and the denial of themselves follow Christ in faith and love and humility, and who possess Him together with the Father and the Spirit within themselves, for them all things are possible and become easy, according to him who said while in the Spirit: "I can do all things in Him Who strengthens me" [Phil 4:13]. Having been made rich with Him, they shall see invisibly the inexpressible beauty of God Himself. They shall hold Him without touching. They shall comprehend incomprehensibly His imageless image, His formless form, His shape without shape which, in sight without seeing and in beauty uncompounded, is ever varied and unchanging.

What is it that, comprehending, they will see? The simple light of divinity, this is what they will see richly with the eyes of their intellect; this what they will also handle, drawn by irresistible love, with immaterial hands; what they will eat without consuming with the spiritual mouth of their intellect and soul. They will never have enough, never be satiated with the contemplation of that beauty, of that sweetness. For, stranger still, the light which wells up in them is always increasing in sweetness and kindling their desire ever the more greatly. And, yet more, if ever it should not appear to them the more piercingly so as to leave them deprived of the whole, or if, though it be but for a little while, it should wish to disappear completely, then it produces in them the sharp and unbearable pain of ineffable longing.

The pauper and the princess: an illustration of sanctified eros[5]

Now, let us try to understand the need and fire of such

5   *Eros* as functional equivalent to *agape* has a long history in the patristic writers. Symeon's sources here are likely Gregory of Nyssa, the *Macarian Homilies*, and Dionysius Areopagita (cf. *Divine Names* IV.10-17). The underlying idea is that the human

longing by way of an example. Imagine with me a young woman who is beloved by a certain poor man. She is of the royal family and crowned with the imperial diadem, is more beautiful than all the women on earth, and she is within her bed chamber. The man who loves her approaches from outside, and he is like one cast off on account of his poverty and extreme lowliness. If the girl, then, were to reach just her hand outside through a small and narrow opening, and give it, covered with gold, to her lover, he would seize it and cover it with kisses, dreaming the while of her incomparable beauty and picturing himself united and reigning with her—as, indeed, she has promised him with many oaths. Then, suddenly, she snatches her hand from between his and withdraws it to herself, and hides it completely. Would this not cause him unbearable sorrow and thereby serve the more to inflame his longing for her? I think it would, and you, too, will agree with my choice of example.

If this sort of thing occurs naturally with regard to bodies that are visible and perceptible, and to things which are corruptible and quickly pass away, think how much the more it must apply to things which are invisible and intelligible, incorruptible and eternal. For, as much as the eternal good things are better than what is temporary, so much the more by analogy do they instill a greater love and longing in the souls of their lovers, whose longing thus for God does not allow them to be held by lust or passion for any object whatsoever. Such people are not drawn by glory or luxury or possessions, neither are

drive usually understood as sexual yearning and as fulfilled in sexual union, is more truly intended by the Creator to impell the human being to communion with Him. That is, *eros* discovers its true purpose in partaking of the uncreated divinity. We have already seen that Symeon is not afraid of the boldest use of sexual imagery—cf. his *Hymn* 15 and our *Introduction,* Part II, in vol. III, forthcoming.

they allowed even in thought any contact with love for bodies. Instead, they are like a bridegroom staring at the colors of his fiance's lifeless portrait. He is attracted to it, sighs continuously, and longs to see her. It kindles his longing and desire for her. And, when he does see her in the flesh, the bride, approaching him, not in the form of the portrait but in her own incomparable and inexpressibly living and spotless beauty, and embraces her and enfolds her in his arms, he can no longer bear his prior attachment to her portrait. The same, and more so, do they also feel who look up from the grandeur and beauty of visible creatures to the power and wisdom of their Maker, and are led progressively up from the former to faith and love for God, and to holy fear. For when they are essentially united with God Himself and are made worthy of seeing and partaking of Him, they are no longer attracted by passions, or affections, or attachments to the images of the Creator in created things, nor at all to the shadows of the visible world. Their thought rests on what is beyond the senses and, being as it were mingled and vested with the radiance of divine nature, it no longer possesses a perception which is oriented toward the visible as before.

Symeon testifies to his own experience of God

Here I will imitate the one who said: "As to one untimely born, He appeared also to me" [I Cor 15:8], for this is the blessed passion that we, too, a cast off, have by God's grace and love for mankind, and by many prayers, been deemed worthy of suffering. We have been taught by Him. We have received by experience, in perception, in vision and in knowledge, everything which we have discussed, and have set this down in writing for the edification and encouragement of all who seek God and long to find Him. Share this our suffering, therefore, and pray with us, all you who have taken edification from the present discourse and who choose to ascend in very deed to these heights, so that, by your acceptable prayers to

God, the coal of divine longing may not only be preserved unquenched in us, but that indeed it may be kindled yet more with flame, and that He keep us pure and blameless and without spot, He Who has ascended from earth to heaven and has glorified our human race. Yes, truly, He will cleave to me and manifestly unite with me, and will make all of me worthy of being mingled consciously with all of Himself, and with you, in a fusion without confusion and a union which escapes expression, for His promises do not lie. To Him is due all glory, honor, and worship, together with the Father and the all-Holy Spirit, now and ever, and unto ages of ages without end. Amen.

FIFTH ETHICAL DISCOURSE

Introduction

Discourse V develops the concluding remarks of the preceding and takes up arms, in a manner altogether characteristic, against "those who say they have the Holy Spirit within themselves unconsciously." Taking his text from Romans 6, Symeon argues that being "clothed with Christ" implies a conscious experience of the Savior. That experience, he continues, was never limited simply to the great figures of the past such as St. Paul or the other Apostles. Christ's words to Phillip, "He who has seen Me has seen the Father" (Jn 14:9), is addressed to every Christian, and St. Paul himself asks his flock to "be imitators of me" (I Cor 4:16 and 11:1). There is, Symeon declares, no envy among the saints, no clinging to special privileges. Citing especially the passages on the Holy Spirit in John 14-16, he argues that the Holy Spirit, Who is God from God, the very light and glory of divinity, is promised to every believer. The argument is summed up by a reference to one of the New Theologian's favorite texts, John 14:21: "...he who loves Me will be loved by My Father, and I will come and manifest Myself to him." Once again, and here in greater detail, Symeon calls his own early experience of the glory to witness. The manifestation Christ speaks of is no mere figure of speech but sober truth, and the believer is to pursue this treasure which is the substance and meaning of the new creation. In an important qualification at the end of the treatise, Symeon does admit that the conscious experience of Christ's presence may not in fact be given to everyone who asks. Still, he insists, everyone is obliged to seek and desire it, and it surely will be given to all who long for it—"either in this age or in the world to come."

ON THOSE WHO SAY THAT THEY POSSESS THE HOLY SPIRIT UNCONSCIOUSLY

Here I am again, writing against those who say they have the Spirit of God unconsciously, who think that they have Him in themselves as a result of divine Baptism and who, while they believe they have this treasure, yet recognize themselves as wholly deaf to Him. I am writing against those who, even while confessing they felt nothing whatever in their baptism, still imagine that the gift of God has indwelt and existed within their soul, unconsciously and insensibly, from that moment up to the present time. Nor are they the only ones, but I am also against those who say they have never had any perception of that gift in contemplation or in revelation, but that they still receive it by faith and thought alone, not by experience, and hold it within themselves as a result of hearing the scriptures.

Only the dead feel nothing: a dialogue with his opponents

Let me begin with their own words and let us see what these men who are wise and experts, at least in their own eyes, have to say: "'As many of you as have been baptized into Christ,' says Paul, 'have put on Christ' [Gal 3:27]. Well then? Are we not baptized, too? And if we are baptized, is it not then also clear that, as the Apostle says, we have put on Christ?" This is their first demonstration and proof.

So what might not we, but the Holy Spirit, say in reply to them? "Very well, you people, then tell us what this garment is. Christ?" "Yes," they say. "Well then, is Christ something or—I speak as a fool to other fools—is He nothing?" "Of course," they would say (if they have not gone completely insane), "He is something." "If therefore you confess Him to be something, then say first of all what He is, so that you may teach yourselves thus to speak like believers, and not unbelievers." "What else," they say, "is Christ, if not perfect God truly become perfect man?" "Since you have confessed this, tell us also why God has become man. Certainly, as the divine Scriptures teach, together with those events which have occurred and daily occur (unless perhaps you ignore them by making yourselves willfully deaf), in order that He may make man god. By what means does He accomplish this? By the divinity or by the flesh?" "Obviously," they say, "by divinity. For 'It is the Spirit that gives life; the flesh is of no avail,' says John [Jn 6:63]." "If then He first deified the flesh which He had assumed with His own divinity, and so quickened us all not by corruptible flesh but by that flesh which had been deified, it was so that we should no longer recognize Him as in any way merely man, but as one God perfect in two natures—for God is one—and the corruptible as swallowed up by incorruption, and the body not as destroyed by that which is bodiless but as wholly changed, remaining unconfused with yet ineffably permeated by and united in unmingled mingling with God Who is Three, so that one God in Father, Son, and Holy Spirit may be worshipped, the Trinity, neither as taking on any addition due to the Economy [Incarnation] nor any passion due to the body."

Why am I saying all this? So that by knowing beforehand what you have confessed to as a result of my questioning, you should not out of ignorance turn aside from the straight path of these thoughts and so be to blame both for effort on our part, and a greater condemnation for your own soul. I will therefore recall for you once again in brief what I have said so that what I am about to say will be quite clear. Christ thus exists. And what is He? True God truly become perfect man. For this reason He became man which before He was not, in order to make man a god which he had never been before. Since He is not divisible, He has deified and made us god by His divinity, and not by His flesh alone. Now pay attention and answer my questions thoughtfully. If the baptized have put on Christ, what is it that they have put on? God. He then who has put on God, will he not recognize with his intellect and see what he has clothed himself with? The man who has clothed his naked body feels the garment that he sees, but the man who is naked in soul will not know that he has put on God? If he who is clothed with God does not perceive Him, what has he put on in fact? According to you, God would be nothing at all. For, if He were something, those putting Him on would know it. When we put nothing on, we feel nothing, but whenever we are clothed by ourselves or by others, so long as our sense are intact, we are quite aware of it. Only the dead feel nothing when they are clothed, and I am very much afraid that those who say such things are the ones who are really and truly dead and naked. So, the question is resolved.

The Christian is called to see God in this life

Then they say: "Paul commands that we 'Quench not the Spirit' [I Thess 5:19]." They reveal their own ignorance by quoting this when they have not understood the sense of the Apostle's words. When someone says to another; "Do not put out the lamp," he is not talking about a lamp which has already been extinguished, but about one which is still burning and emitting light. Once again, we have raised an objection to them here.

What then? Do you people then see the Spirit wholly within yourselves, burning and shining as is proper to Him? Not only do they not reply to this, but their faces immediately change expression and turn away. They start to make trouble, as if they had heard a blasphemy. Then, with a show of honoring their interrogator and pretending to be meek, they reply (not without sharpness): "And who would ever dare say they saw Him or could see Him at all? You must stop this! Scripture says: 'No one has ever seen God' [Jn 1:18]." O! what darkness! So tell us, who said what follows? "The only-begotten," the same text adds, "Who is in the bosom of the Father, He has made Him known" [Jn 1:18]. You speak truly but, though your witness is true, it is in despite of your own soul. If I could show you the same Son of God telling you that this is possible, what would you say then? Because He does say: "He who has seen Me has seen the Father" [Jn 14:9], and He did not say this meaning the [physical] sight of His flesh, but the revelation of His divinity. If we were to suppose that this was said in reference to His body, then those who crucified Him also saw the Father, and there would be no difference or preference between believers and unbelievers, but everyone would evidently have arrived equally—and will arrive—at the desired beatitude. But this is not so, not at all, as He makes quite clear in His discussions with the Jews when He says: "If you had known Me, you would have know my Father also" [Jn 14:7].

That it is possible for us to look upon God, insofar as men are able to see at all, listen once more to Christ, the Son of God Himself, when He says: "Blessed are the pure in heart, for they shall see God" [Mt 5:8]. So what do you have to say to that? I am aware, however, that the man who does not believe in the good things which he has in his very hands and makes no attempt to seize them will take refuge in the future, and so will reply: "Yes, certainly the pure in heart will see God, but this will happen only in the future, not in the present age." My dear friend, just why or how will this happen? If He said that God will be seen by purity of heart, then clearly when this purity comes to pass the vision will follow in consequence. And, if you had ever purified your heart, you would know that what is said is true, but, since you have not taken this to heart nor believed that it was true, you have accordingly also despised that purity and completely failed to obtain the vision. For if the purification takes place in this life, then so does the vision. On the other hand, if you should say that the seeing is for after death, then you certainly posit the purification as also after death, and thus it will turn out that you will never see God since after death there will be no work for you by which you might find purification.

However, what else does the Lord say? "He who loves Me will keep My commandments, and I will love him and manifest Myself to Him" [Jn 14:21]. So when will this manifestation occur? In this life or the future one? It is clear that He means the present life. For wherever the commandments are kept exactly, there, too, is the manifestation of the Savior, and it is after the manifestation that perfect love comes to pass in us. If the latter does not occur, then we are able neither to believe in, nor love Him as we ought, since it is written: "[Can] he who does not love his brother whom he has seen, love God Whom he has not seen" [I Jn 4:20]? In no way!

There is no envy among saints. All are called to share the experience of St. Paul

Thus he who is unable to love is obviously unable to believe either. Listen also to Paul saying the same thing: "So faith, hope, love abide, these three; but the greatest of these is love" [I Cor 13:13]. If faith is yoked with hope, and hope consequent upon love, he who does not love does not possess hope, and, being without hope, he is also clearly devoid of faith. For how could love possibly be present when its causes are absent? As the roof of a house will not stand without foundations, neither is it possible to find the love of God in a human soul which is without faith and a sure hope. Nor will he who does not have love be edified by any of the remaining virtues, or be at all profited without it, just as Paul himself also bears witness in his writing. And on seeing God beginning with this life, listen to him again when he says: "Now I see in a mirror and dimly, but then face to face," and once more: "Now I know in part, but then I shall know even as I have been known" [I Cor 13:12]. "But," says my interlocuter, "that was Paul!" Well, was not Paul a human being in every respect, a fellow servant, and like us in his passions? "But who is Paul's equal, you proud and shameless fellow," he says, "that you should equate him with us men?" To which people Paul himself—and not we—cries out with a loud voice and says the following: "Christ came to save sinners"—listen well!—"of whom I am first" [I Tim 1:15]. He is thus the first of the sinners who are being saved. You should become the second, or third, or tenth. Become, if you like, a fellow soul with the thousands or ten thousands, and you will have ranked yourself with Paul. You will also do him honor, as he says himself: "Be imitators of me as I am of Christ" [I Cor 11:1]; and again: "I wish that all were as I am myself" [I Cor 7:7].

So if you want to praise Paul or honor him, imitate him; and whatever he is, you should also become such by faith, and then you will honor him while he in turn will welcome you and reckon you worthy of the same glory and crown of boasting as he, because you will have been convinced by his words and followed him, and will have become yourself his imitator and his equal. But if you say that it dishonors Paul for another to become his equal, and for this reason you hold your salvation in contempt and neglect it, then know that he will reject you as having reasoned wrongly and will thus himself abominate you. Would you like me to show you then that you will honor him still more greatly, and make him rejoice, and glorify him, if you are able to become greater than he and still more akin to God? Listen to him advancing this idea and saying: "I could wish that I myself were accursed and cut off from Christ for the sake of my brethren, my kinsmen by race" [Rom 9:3]. He is perfectly ready to be cut off from Christ in order that you be saved, and you say that he will think it a dishonor if I should want and strive to become such as he? No, my brother, there is no envy in God's holy ones. Among them there is neither lust nor appetite for precedence or superior glory. For the saints and those who generation after generation show themselves friends and prophets of God there is a single precedence of seating and preference of position, and glory, and rest, and delight: to see God. Those who see Him are delivered from any kind of curiosity. They neither look nor turn toward anything in this life, nor to any others among men, nor are they able even to conceive of anything incongruous, but have instead been liberated from everything that is relative. So, too, do they abide, forever unchanging and unmoved with respect to evil.

Hearsay is not enough. The saints describe what they have seen

However, now I will ask you something and you will answer me intelligently. Those who have written about these matters, from where do they get their knowledge? And he who writes now, whence does he know? Tell me, so that I not give you again the impression of talking vaingloriously, whose are these words? Take careful counsel and surely you will come to some conclusion and deliver me from disputations. "They come from a man, certainly," he says. O my! The vision does not come to you by hearing, does it? Rather, you remain one who hears and sees nothing at all. You say these words come from a man? If they do, then you are obliged to say how they do, since a man is incapable of knowing or expressing not only someone else's reasonings and moods, but even the impulses and states of an animal's being. With regard to the inner state of a soul, "What person knows a man's thoughts except the spirit of the man which is within him?" [I Cor 2:11]. And if it is difficult for one man to know well the impulses and conditions of another man, and even of irrational animals, where or how is it possible for anyone to know what is from God, I mean, the change and condition which is effected in the saints as a result of the vision of Him, not to speak for now of the activity which accomplishes it? But in particular, if the words are a man's then clearly so are the concepts. With respect to these matters, however, the concept ought not to be called a concept, but instead a vision of what truly exists, because we speak from that vision, and one ought rather to call what is said an account of things which have been seen. A concept or thought, on the other hand, is properly spoken of as concerning something non-existent, or as a purpose which is born of the mind's intention, such as to do something good or bad which we have not yet actually done, and from the thought one is led to action such that the thought becomes the principle of our future deed, as in: "First God conceives the angelic and heavenly powers, and the thought was deed."[1]

Consider, then, that all our words and explanations concerning these matters are not about some non-existent and uncertain things, but instead concern what has already taken place, and will take place in the future, and that they derive from the vision and contemplation of these things. Someone who explains something about, for example, a house or a city or a place and its arrangement and condition, or again, about some theater and what goes on inside it, is obliged first of all to have seen the places and have learned well about them, and then afterwards to speak carefully and accurately about what he wants to cover. If he were not to have seen it beforehand, then what in fact could he really say about it? What notion regarding something he had not seen at all could he otherwise provide for his account? Tell me, what consideration or clev-

1 Gregory of Nazianzus, Or. 38.9, PG 36.320.

erness or learning, and what wisdom, thought, notion or rationale could he reasonably find to discourse on something he does not know? To say anything about matters which one knows nothing about or has not seen is obviously unreasonable and ill-bred. Therefore if no one is able to talk or lecture about visible and earthly things unless he has been an eyewitness to them, how, O my brothers, could anyone be empowered to talk or lecture about God and the things of God, or even the saints and servants of God, and the nature of that relationship which the latter have with God, and about what sort of vision of God it is which comes ineffably to pass in them? It is that vision which spiritually introduces into their hearts an inexpressible activity, concerning which human speech does not allow one to say anything more unless one has first been enlightened with the light of knowledge, in accordance with the tenor of the commandment [cf. Hos 10:12].

But, that we may lead you to the light in every respect, when you hear "light of knowledge," do not imagine that this is mere knowledge of what is said and no light at all. The prophet did not say an "account" or "lecture about light," but "light of knowledge" and "of knowledge light" [Hos 10:12]. There is no other way for anyone to know about God unless it is by means of the contemplation of the light which is sent by Him. It is just as in the case of someone who is telling some others about some man or city. He first talks to them about what he has seen and heard. His listeners, who have not seen either the man or city about which they are hearing, cannot by merely hearing about them know them in the same way as the man who has actually seen them and is telling them about it. It is just the same with regard to the Jerusalem on high and the invisible God Who dwells within it, or concerning the unapproachable glory of His countenance, or about the energy and power of His all-Holy Spirit—in other words, His light. No one can say anything unless he has first seen the light with the eyes of his soul and knows precisely its illuminations and activities as they occur within himself. But if in the Holy Scripture he should hear something from those who speak of seeing God, then it is uniquely through the Holy Spirit that he is taught about these things. Thus neither again is he able to say that "I am come to knowledge of God by this act of hearing alone." For how can he have received knowledge of what he has not seen? If seeing alone does not suffice to cause in us complete knowledge of what is seen, how could merely hearing bring about the knowledge of God in us? God is light and the vision of Him is as light. Thus, in the vision of the light there is knowledge first of all that God is, just as in the case of a man there is first hearing about him, then sight of him, and with the sight of him the knowledge that the man about whom one has heard does in fact exist. Nor does the matter stop here. While someone may tell you about a man, when you see him you are unable to know for sure who he is and be assured that this is he about whom you have learned by mere hearing. Instead, your soul is divided by doubt, and either you ask him himself or someone who knows him, and so learn for certain that this indeed is he.

Symeon's own experience and its confirmation by his elder[2]

This, invariably, is just what occurs concerning the invisible God. Whenever someone sees Him revealed, he sees light. While on the one hand he is amazed at what he has seen, on the other he does not know immediately who it is who has appeared, yet he dares not ask Him. And how could he? He is unable even to lift up his eyes and look on that grandeur. With fear and trembling he looks instead, as it were, at his own feet,

2 See C 16.78-144 (deC, 200-202), as well as our Introduction, Part I, in vol. III, forthcoming.

knowing fully only that it is Someone Who has appeared before his face. And if there happens to be some other man who has told him beforehand about such things, as having known God from before, he goes to this man and says: "I have seen." And the other says: "What did you see, child?" "Light, O my father, so sweet, sweet! So much so, father, that my reason has not the strength to tell you." And, while he is saying this, his heart leaps and pounds, and catches on fire with longing for what he has seen. Then, with many warm tears, he begins to say again: "That light, father, appeared to me. The walls of my cell immediately vanished and the world disappeared, fleeing I think from before His face, and I remained alone in the presence alone[3] of the light. And I do not know, father, if this my body was there, too. I do not know if I was outside of it. For awhile I did not know that I carry and am clothed with a body. And such great joy was in me and is with me now, great love and longing both, that I was moved to streams of tears like rivers, just like now as you see." The other then answers and says: "It is He, child." And, at this word, he sees Him again and, little by little, comes to be completely purified and, purified, grows bold and asks that One Himself, and says: "My God, is it You?" And He answers and says: "Yes, I am He, God, Who for your sake became man; and behold, I have made you, as you see, and shall make you, god."

The taste of future blessings brings understanding

When he has spent time in contrition, in weeping, in prostrations, and in humbling himself, he begins little by little to know the things of God, and it is when he has reached this point

3   The double "alone," "alone to the Alone," is a borrowing from
    Plotinus (*Enneads* VI.7,34), though almost certianly not a direct
    one but via the tradition of spiritual writings where it had become
    a commonplace. On the frequency of this expression in Symeon's
    works, see our Introduction, Part II, in vol. III, forthcoming.

that he learns "His will, which is holy and acceptable and perfect" [Rom 12:2]. To repeat myself, if he were not to have seen Him, neither would he be able to know Him; and unless he knows Him, how would he be able to know His holy will? If such is impossible with respect to human beings, it applies all the more to God. Thus, while progressing and becoming still more conformed to God, he knows from what God does in him what He also did with all the saints who preceded him, and what He is going to do with those who come after. He is taught about the crowns and rewards which are to come. On the one hand, he is initiated by God Himself, in that he clearly perceives that these things are beyond intellect and reason and thought, while on the other, he also understands clearly what state he and those with him will have after the resurrection. No, he does not enjoy these things in the present life, even if some people have maliciously represented us as saying as much. Since, in supposing ourselves to be enjoying everthing herebelow, we would then—according to those others—be denying the resurrection itself, the judgement and retribution, and willfully throwing away our hope of things to come. But we think and say no such thing. Rather, we vehemently anathematize those people who do say it. Therefore, while we do confess and say that we already enjoy in some measure the pledge of those good things while still in this life, we hope to receive the whole after death, as it is written: "Now," he says, "I know in part, but when the whole shall come, then that which is partial shall be done away" [cf. I Cor 13:10 and 12]; and elsewhere: "We are God's children now, and it does not yet appear what we shall be; but we know that when He appears, we shall be like Him" [I Jn 3:2].

Proceeding with our inquiry by way of question and answer, let us as it were ask the man who just wrote what we saw above: "O friend and beloved of Christ, where from do you

know that you will be like Him? Tell us, from where?" "From
the Spirit," he says, "Whom He has given us. It is from Him
that we know that we are children of God and that God Himself
is within us, since He Himself also said these things to me in a
mystical voice." Now, let us return to our subject.

Through the Holy Spirit the saints become eyewitnesses of the world to come.[4]

We said above that it is right to call those things our
thoughts or concepts whenever a notion concerning something
good is formed in our mind, as for example that I should
acquire something or do good or evil to someone, but that we
call it an explanation and not a thought or concept when it
concerns something which has already occurred or which we
have seen. Then we asked the following: how can someone talk
about some object, or cities, or theaters, or people whom he has
not seen, or describe their appearance, or form, or place? And,
if he were to talk about it anyway, his listeners would rightly
call him a teller of fairytales. The prophets and apostles, therefore, who have spoken about the Day of the Lord and His
dreadful and glorious coming again, and said that it will be like
a thief in the night or like the birth-pangs of a woman in
labor—where did they learn these things? It was obviously
either from having heard them from someone else, or from
having become eyewitnesses of that Day. If they had not seen
it, or not heard someone else telling about it, how could they
have said anything? If then they heard about it—since I am not
yet saying that they saw it and then spoke of it, but just that they
heard of it—tell me, from whom did they hear it? You know it
all, so tell me, from where did they learn of it? But, if you do
not know what to say, then listen and know that they learned it
from the Holy Spirit, just as, indeed, the Lord said to them:

4   See Discourse X, vol.I, pp. 141-170.

> But when the Counselor comes [Jn 15:26] ...the Holy
> Spirit, Whom the Father will send in My name, He will
> teach you all things, and will bring to your remem-
> brance all that I have said to you [Jn 14:26].

And that the Holy Spirit, when He had descended upon the
Apostles, said and taught them the things which Christ had not
yet said to them, the same Evangelist says:

> I have yet many things to say to you, but you cannot
> bear them now. When the Spirit of truth comes, He will
> guide you into all the truth; for He will not speak on His
> own authority, but whatever He hears He will speak,
> and He will declare to you the things that are to come.
> He will glorify Me, for He will take what is Mine and
> declare it to you [Jn 16:12-14].

You have learned from what source they were taught who wrote
about that Day and the manifestation of the Lord, and about
what is stored up and going to happen to the sinners and the
righteous. Thus, illumined by the Holy Spirit, they at once saw
and wrote about all the rest of those things which we do not see.

But answer this question: What is the Holy Spirit? "God," you
say, "we confess Him as true God from true God." Thus, as you
see and in accordance with the dogmas of the Church, you say that
He is God. So, too, by both saying and thinking that He is true
God proceeding from true God, you establish that those who have
the Holy Spirit have confessedly God dwelling always within
themselves, just as Christ said to the Apostles:

> If you love Me, you will keep My commandments. And
> I will pray the Father, and He will give you another
> Counselor, to be with you forever [Jn 14:15-16].

So, now you have learned that He both abides and dwells within
them for ages without end, since to say "be with you forever"
indicates that He is everlastingly and unendingly with them
and, both in the present and in the age to come, is inseparable

from them. And, that both the divine Apostles and all who have
been made worthy of receiving Him have seen the Holy Spirit,
listen to what follows:

> The Spirit of truth, Whom the world cannot receive,
> because it neither sees Him nor knows Him; you know
> Him, for He dwells within you, and will be in you [Jn
> 14:17].

And that you may know that those who love Him and keep His
commandments also see Christ, listen to same Lord Himself
when He says:

> He Who has my commandments and keeps them, he it
> is who loves Me; and he who loves Me will be loved by
> My Father, and I will love him and manifest Myself to
> him [Jn 14:21].

Let it therefore be known to every Christian that Christ does
not lie, that He is true God and confessedly manifests Himself to
those who show their love for Him by keeping His commandments, as He Himself says, and that through His manifestation the
Holy Spirit is given to them, and that, through the Holy Spirit, the
Father Himself in turn abides with them inseparably. Such as they
are, the saints say nothing of themselves. Whoever does say that
they say anything of themselves says that it is possible for a man
to know, by the same method, what is proper both to men and to
God. Or, if this is not the case, then he is instead obviously calling
liars and tellers of fairy stories those who speak by the Holy Spirit.
He says that they are not taught by Him, but teach others by way
of their own reasoning about what they have neither seen nor
heard. To the contrary, we must realize that if these are in accord
and speak with the God-bearing fathers who have gone before, [5]
then clearly they, too, speak in the same Spirit, and that those who

5   Note that Symeon lays down the harmony of one's experience
    with the tradition as an essential criterion for distinguishing
    the true from the false charismatic.

disbelieve them, and even slander them, sin against the One Who speaks through them.

An Exhortation to pray for the gift of the Spirit, and a warning not to presume to leadership without Him

You have thus learned, beloved, that the Kingdom of God is within you; that, if you desire it, all the eternal good things are also in your hands. Therefore hurry and see, and receive, and hold within yourself the good things which are stored up, and take care lest, by thinking you possess them already, you be deprived of all of them. Weep and make prostrations. As the blind man once said, so should you say even now: "Have mercy on me, Son of David, and open the eyes of my soul, so that I may see the light of the world, even You, Who are God, and may become, even I, a son of the day; and so that You may not abandon me, O Good One, as unworthy and without a share in Your divinity. Lord, manifest Yourself to me, so that I may know that You have loved me as one who has kept, Master, Your divine commandments. O Merciful One, send the Comforter even to me, so that He may teach me the things concerning You; and, O God of all, declare what is Yours to me. Illumine me with the true light, O Compassionate One, so that I may see the glory which You had with Your Father before the world was made. Abide even in me, as You have said, so that I, too, may become worthy of abiding in You, and may then consciously enter into You and consciously possess You within myself. O Invisible One, take form in me so that, beholding Your impossible beauty, I may be clothed, O Heavenly One, with Your image and forget all things visible. Compassionate One, give me that glory which the Father gave You, so that I may, as all of Your servants, become god by grace and be ever with You, now and always and for ages without end. Amen."

Yes, my dear friend, believe and be persuaded that this is so and that this is our faith. Believe it, brother. This is what it is to be regenerated and renewed and live that life which is in

Christ. Do you not hear Basil the Great saying in his exhortation for the feast of lights: "Do you not, O man, long to see
yourself become a young man from one who was old"[6] And
Paul says: "If anyone is in Christ, he is a new creation; the old
has passed away, behold, all things are become new" [II Cor
5:17]. What does he mean then by saying "all things?" Tell me,
you, tell me! Is it heaven which has been changed? The earth?
Is it rather the sun, or stars, or sea, or any visible thing which
has become new and fresh? But you cannot say that, since it is
to and about us that this is written. For being dead, we were
raised up to life; corruptible, we are made over into incorruption; mortal, and we are changed over into immortality;
earthly, and we are become heavenly; fleshly and possessing
our birth from the flesh, we are become spiritual, are reborn
and created anew by the Holy Spirit.

Brothers, this is the new creation in Christ. This is what is
accomplished and takes place daily in the true faithful and
chosen ones. While yet in the body, as we have often said, they
become conscious partakers, in part, of all these things. Nor is
this all, but, indeed, after death they hope to inherit these things
completely and assuredly. I mean that then they will enter
completely into the fullness of those good things in which they
even now commune. For, if we always teach that we eat and
drink Christ, are clothed with and see Him and are seen by
Him, and know also that we have Him in us and in turn that we
abide in Him, that while He dwells in us we also dwell in Him,
that is, that He is become our house as we in turn have become
His, and then that we are also His sons while He becomes our
father, and that He is light shining in darkness and we say that
we see Him—as, according to Scripture, "The people who sat
in darkness saw a great light" [Is 9:2]—if we then say that all
this and the rest that we have said, all of which is clearly taught

6   PG 31.432D.

in holy Scripture as occurring in us even during this present life, does not in fact occur in us, or that if it does, it does so "mystically and imperceptibly" in such a way that we know nothing about it, then how are we different from the dead?

God forbid that by giving yourselves to such unbelief you go down to the depths of damnation. Rather, even if you had no hope until now of acquiring any perception of such things and for that reason asked for nothing, then be completely assured by this work before you. Believe first of all that these things are true and in accordance with the holy Scriptures and, by studying the latter thoroughly, know that here, already, the seal of the Holy Spirit is given to those who believe. And, having believed, pursue it so that you may obtain it; fight for it, but not like someone who merely bats at the air. "Ask," for this "and it will be given you; knock, and it will be opened to you" [Mt 7:7], either in this world or in the world to come. Meanwhile, learn; meanwhile, repent, submit yourself, fast, weep, pray. Then, by these means and others like them: run, fight, pursue, seek, knock, ask, and incline toward nothing else until you have obtained it; until you seize it by the hand; until you take it; until it is opened to you and you enter within; until you hear: "Well done, good and faithful servant; you have been faithful over a little, I will set you over much" [Mt 25:21]; until you have become children of the light and of the day. But take care lest, before you have seen and received and experienced these things, you fool yourselves into thinking that you are something who are nothing, such that, having fallen away in your conscience, you suppose yourselves to be spiritual before you have received the Holy Spirit and for this reason rush foolishly to give yourselves up instead to alien thoughts, and advance to abbacies and governerships, and dare to take on the priesthood without fear, and devote yourselves shamelessly and through endless plotting to the acquisition of metropolitanates and episcopates in order to shepherd the Lord's people. I beg you instead, pay attention to yourselves. Keep in mind what is above and seek it, long for it, and pay mind to nothing earthly before you have received those good things.

Yes, I indeed pray your charity,[7] let us hold in contempt everything visible. Let us shake off from ourselves everything which is merely human. Let us abominate everything impassioned and injurious, so that we may attain to the good things of this present life and of the one to come, in Christ Jesus our Lord, to Whom is due all glory, honor, and worship, together with the Father Who is without beginning, and the all-Holy, good, and life-creating Spirit, the one unique and thrice-holy light, now and ever, and unto ages of ages. Amen.

---

7   See page 15, note 2 above.

SIXTH ETHICAL DISCOURSE

Introduction

Discourse VI returns to the question of dispassion. Here we find Symeon again defending the possibility of freedom from the passions in the present life. He is led to this insistence because of the rumors surrounding his elder, Symeon the Pious (who remains unnamed), as a result of the latter's unconventional behavior, which included association with people of dubious repute, women among them, outside his monastery. To be sure, our Symeon admits, one is obliged to eschew such contacts while still engaged in the ascetic struggle and not yet perfected. The person who seeks God wholeheartedly, however, will find Him and, in the finding, be transformed. God the Word became flesh and thus transfigured both the human soul and body. As a result, whoever has truly experienced Christ becomes himself or herself transformed. Such a person, clothed body and soul with the Holy Spirit, cannot be soiled. Freed from the passions and with the eyes of the soul thus cleansed and illumined, he or she sees through the allure of material things to the truth beneath. Only the illumined saint can be a true physician of souls. Only such a person is capable of the detachment necessary to regard the passions of another, as a doctor examines a diseased body and prescribes the proper treatment without falling victim himself, or herself, to the illness. Such a one is the true, the only true, imitator of Christ, the lover of humankind. From defense, Symeon turns at the end of the treatise to attack and warning. If you have not known this transformation, he tells his opponents, you have no more business pretending to authority in the spiritual life than a worldly man has of proclaiming himself a magistrate without the Emperor's writ. Such pretension brings down upon itself a just and terrible retribution.

ON DISPASSION AND A VIRTUOUS LIFE

Freedom from the passions is possible in this life[1]

Having often conversed with many people in the world, I have heard almost all of them say during the course of discussions over certain matters (I mean about passion and dispassion)—and not just from people who are imperfect in virtue and piety, but also from those who fancy they are perfect in virtue and who have reputations and great fame in the world—that it is not possible for a man to arrive at such a height of humility that he may converse and dine with a woman without yielding to some injury or suffering in secret from some kind of impulse or stain. When I had heard them myself, I was filled with despondency and felt compelled to mourn for people who say such things and to weep for them out of sympathy. I know precisely that they could not otherwise have said what they did unless it were out of great ignorance of God's gifts. For, unless they were deprived of the true dispassion and covered by the darkness of the passions, and had become slaves of pleasures and the wishes of the flesh, they would not have been ignorant of the life-giving mortification of Jesus our God and disbelieved in it.

How, indeed, shall such people ever believe that there are in fact certain others who are—or are becoming—dead to the world, and who are living that life which is alone in the Spirit?

---

1   The following passages call on Symeon's recollections of his elder, Symeon the Pious. He is here obviously seeking to defend his master's reputation—though he nowhere names him in this Discourse.

Throughout their lives the former group have put their emphasis on doing everything by hypocrisy for the purpose of pleasing men and being called by them friends of God. They imagine they have achieved dispassion while in the midst of passions, themselves being and becoming wholly sin. While they convince themselves that human praise alone suffices for virtue and holiness—thus denying dispassion—they want to be and are called holy without it, as if they could possess holiness solely by virtue of that human praise. They judge someone unworthy of any consideration if it chances simply that he is not praised by the many. It seems they are unaware that one man who knows God and is known by Him is greater than myriads of unbelievers who do not know Him, even if the latter should happen to be praised and blessed by the whole world, just like one man who can see is better than an infinite multitude of the blind. All Scripture and history bear witness that it is possible for someone among those who truly struggle to arrive at such great freedom and, having become once for all a participant of God's grace, to attain to a dispassion of soul and body such that, not only does he remain untroubled and dispassionate while dining and conversing with women, but suffers moreover no injury while circulating in the middle of towns, and hearing singers and guitar players, and seeing people laughing and dancing and amusing themselves. The acts of the saints provide us with such testimonies, and the pious engage in every ascetic practice and mortification precisely for the sake of this blessed condition.

Flee the world! Counsel to monastic ascesis[2]

The goal of those who do battle in godly manner is there-

2 Note that Symeon presupposes a monastic setting here: the abandonment of relatives, mortifications, obedience, the rule of prayer, etc. are all features of the monastic life. Whether monastic or lay, however, his point is double: the struggle

fore this, to flee the world first of all and everything in it. I mean by "world" the present life, that is, this passing age, and by what is "in the world" everything around us which the Word has commanded us to abandon and from which we are thus obliged to flee, such as father and mother, siblings and relatives and friends, and, again, from possessions and money and property and every kind of wealth. Not that these things are in themselves forbidden or injurious, but because we are unable to be freed of a passionate attachment to them while living in their midst. For unless he who has already mingled with the pleasures flees from their causes and distances himself from them, he will not be delivered from their lusts. Then, after he has been stripped of all attachments, he ought, if he is serious, deny himself his own soul itself. Thus he is set aright by the mortification of his own will. I am not just talking about what concerns the outer man, such as not eating, not drinking, not doing something lightheartedly, not sleeping, not doing anything which is apparently good without a command to do so, but I mean as well the mortification of what is within, of the heart's own movement, such as not looking with passion at, or greeting anyone or anything in such manner, nor laying blame secretly, nor judging anyone, nor rejoicing at the fall of anyone, nor being angry in thought, nor envying maliciously, nor being jealous with malice.

How shall I ennumerate all the characteristics of piety in order to show you exactly what it is, strictly, to be a Christian? Listen once again to what is proper to life-giving mortification: not hiding even any passing evil thought [from your spiritual father]; not going through even one single day, so far as possible, without tears; not rubbing your face with water as is the custom; not trimming or arranging your hair or beard; not

_____

(*ascesis*) is necessary for everyone but, secondly, it is not itself the point. The goal is always union with God.

undoing your belt before turning in to sleep, so that you are not softened by sleeping more than necessary; not putting your hand within your clothing in order to scratch, but instead protecting yourself from other kinds of touching; not looking directly at the face even of someone who is old (for the agent of evil is everywhere present); not agreeing with anyone against anyone else; not saying anything which is not edifying; not being silent about anything which ought to be said; nor ever abandoning your rule [of prayer] until death; nor having a special friendship with anyone, even if he seems to have the character of a saint; not caring in part or at all about the adornment of your clothes beyond what is decent and proper; not tasting or eating anything with pleasure which your sight has offered as pleasing to the soul. In all these and in still other ways, he who struggles practices continence, but, if he proceeds lazily and negligently in these things, he is following his own will by the hour, even if other people praise him as one who has renounced the world. For while someone may be practising continence in outward things which are visible to everyone and be proclaimed a real practioner by those who do not know how to see, if he is just fulfilling the hidden desires of his heart, then he is hated by God and rejected as impure. Even if he were to spend a thousand years thus in his struggles he would find no profit at all in them if they were merely exterior.

One with God in both soul and body: the whole man is deified.

On the other hand, he who is continent in every respect and has trained his soul not to wander in disorderly manner, nor to follow its own will in any of the ways which are displeasing to God, but instead ardently compels it to traverse, like an acrobat on the high wire, all of God's ordinances, this man will shortly find Him Who is hidden within His divine commandments. And, when he meets Him, forgetting every other activity, he will be astounded. Prostrate before Him, he will have no other desire than to look upon Him. And, when He hides from his sight, the man, perplexed, begins again the way upwards and runs the more strongly, more intensely, more securely. He watches his feet. He walks with care. His memory is aflame, burning with longing, kindled by the hope that he will see Him once more. And when, after having run much, he becomes worn out and unable to complete the course, it is then that he sees the One Whom he pursues, and attains to Him Who had fled from him, and lays hold on the One longed for, and departs wholly from the world and forgets it altogether. He is joined to the angels, mingled with the light, tastes of life, is woven into immortality, enters the enjoyment of delight, ascends to the third heaven, is caught up into paradise, hears ineffable words [cf. II Cor. 12:14], enters the bridal chamber, arrives at the bridal bed, sees the Bridegroom, partakes of the spiritual marriage, is filled by the mystical cup, by the fatted calf, by the living bread, by the drink of life, by the Lamb without spot, by the manna of the intellect. He enters into the enjoyment of all those good things on which even the angelic powers dare not gaze.

In this condition he burns with the Spirit and becomes in his soul wholly a flame. He also shares this radiance with his body, in the way that visible fire shares its own nature with molten iron, and, as the theologian has said,[3] the soul becomes for the body what God has become for the soul. For as the soul is unable to live without being illumined by the Creator, neither does the body live without being empowered by the soul. Attend to the precise meaning of these words: body, soul, and God, these three. God without beginning, without end, unapproachable, unsearchable, invisible, ineffable, intangible, untouchable, dispassionate, inexpressible, has appeared to us in

3   Gregory Nazianzus, *Or.* 2.17; *PG* 35.428A.

these last days in the flesh through His Son, has, we believe, been made known to us through His all-Holy Spirit as like us in every way save sin, has mingled Himself with a rational soul, as someone has said,[4] for the sake of my soul in order to save my spirit and make my flesh immortal. This is what He has in fact promised, saying: "I will dwell in them and walk among them" [II Cor 6:16]; and: "I and My Father... will come to them and make our home with them" [Jn 14:23], that is, with those who believe and give proof of their faith by the works which we have spoken of above. However, pay attention! When God, in accordance with His promises which do not lie, dwells in us, His true servants, and through the activities and illuminations of the all-Holy Spirit walks within our souls, we believe and confess that the worthy souls of such people are inseparable from God. As the soul extends throughout the whole body and no part of the latter lacks its share, so is it necessary that the flesh in turn, being inseparable from the soul—indeed, unable even to live without it—be wholly directed by the soul's will; and, as it is not possible for a body to live without a soul, neither can the body in that case have a will which is foreign to the soul.

We have thus demonstrated that, just as God is unconfusedly and indivisibly worshipped in the Father, Son, and Holy Spirit, so in turn does man, without confusion or division, become in God a god by grace in both his soul and body. The body is not changed into soul, nor the soul transformed into divinity, nor is God confused with the soul, but God remains what He is as God, and the soul what it is by nature, and the body such as it was fashioned, of clay. He who has paradoxically bound all these together, Who has mingled what is both intelligible and immaterial with clay, unites Himself unconfusedly with both of these, and I myself am in His image and

4   Gregory Nazianzus, *Or*. 45:9; *PG* 36.683BC.

likeness, as this discourse has proven. However, if you please, let us continue with our argument since, being moved by pleasure and joy, I would like to remain a while in what has been said in order to set out the meaning of these matters a little more clearly. Father, Son, and Holy Spirit are the one God Whom we worship. Body, soul, and God are the man who is created according to the image of God and made worthy of becoming god.

Therefore the saint is free of passions while in the midst of temptations

Why have I extended my argument to such lengths, and for what purpose in such detail? It is in order that they should be ashamed, or rather, that they who do not possess what is according to the image should recognize themselves, and that they who are separated from God should weep for themselves and know of what things they are deprived, and understand by listening to this discourse what things they are which possess them, and discern what sort of darkness it is which covers them, and tremble at teaching about God! Or better, to put it more charitably, it is in order that they should be horrified at contradicting those who do possess God's grace within themselves, and are taught all things by it, and are enabled to do all things by virtue of it, and that they should stop saying that it is not possible for someone who lives according to God to circulate in the world and dine with women, or converse with them, and remain unsoiled both in his intellect and his perceptions. God is without passion. He is not passionately inclined toward visible things. Now, I know that those who are unable to see with the eyes of the soul or perceive with its senses, who do not understand the thrust of what we have said, will reply with something like this: "While we know that God is without passion, it is not God that we have doubts about, but man."

But it is just for this reason that our argument has anticipated them and shut their mouths by stating that man becomes god by grace, that is, by the gift of the all-Holy Spirit. For just as it is not possible for the sun ever to soil its rays by shining on a swamp, neither is it possible to soil the soul or reasoning faculty of a man who has received the grace to bear God even if his most pure body should chance to be wallowing, so to speak, in a swamp of human bodies—a situation, to be sure, which is unusual for God-fearing people. Nor do I stop there, but even if such a man were to be confined with tens of thousands who were unbelieving and impious and debauched, and his naked body were to be in contact with their naked bodies, he would not be injured in his faith, nor estranged from his Master, nor forgetful of His beauty. Many such things have happened to the martyrs and saints, for example the martyr Chrysanthes and certain others of the saints,[5] yet they were not injured in any way by this machination of the devil because they had God dwelling and abiding within themselves.

The saint is restored to the "image and likeness of God"— Gen 1:26—and sees truly

Whether someone has preserved within himself that which is "according to the image and likeness" from the beginning, or has been recalled to and recovered it, in either case he is thus in possession of the faculty of natural sight. Such a man therefore goes about his life in becoming fashion as in broad daylight. He sees everything for what it is by nature. He does not wonder at the surface glitter of things, but beholds their essence and quality and so remains unmoved, paying attention

5 The feast of SS. Crysanthus and Daria is celebrated on March 19th. If the office in Symeon's day was like contemporary monastic services (and in all essentials it was), then it would have featured in the morning the reading of a synopsis of the lives of the saints of the day. The New Theologian is presupposing, therefore, an audience for whom these lives would have been quite familiar.

only to what is stable and enduring. He sees gold and pays no mind to its gleaming, but understands that it is stuff which comes from the earth and is mere stone and dust, incapable of ever being changed into anything else. He sees silver, pearls, all the precious stones, and his perception is not stolen away by their lovely colors, but he sees them all as stones like any other stone, and reckons them all together as clay. He sees valuable, silken robes and is not amazed by their embroidery, but considers that they are merely the dung of worms, and he pities those who delight in them and seek to acquire them as something precious. He sees someone who is acclaimed, seated on a throne and escorted by many people in solemn procession down the street, or puffed-up with pride, and is disposed to regard it all as a dream. He smiles and is astonished at men's ignorance. He sees the world and lives and walks in the middle of a great city—the Lord is my witness Who works these things in us—as if he were alone in all the world, and he lives with men as if he were in a trackless wilderness, and as if he had nothing to do with anyone or knew no man on earth. Thus is such a man disposed to live.

When therefore this man sees a woman who has a beautiful body, he does not see the blossoming beauty of her face, but sees her instead as rot and mud, as already dying and having become entirely what she is indeed in process of becoming. His intellect would never admire her outward bloom, but sees instead the material corruption which exists within, of which the whole body is composed. For what is a body other than the juice of masticated food? And, even if he were to wish to consider her outward beauty, he knows how to wonder at the Maker in proportion to His works and not to worship the creature rather than the Creator. For thus he recognizes the Maker, from the grandeur and beauty of His works, and his mind is led upwards to the contemplation of Him, and his soul is kindled toward the knowledge of Him. At once he is moved to divine longing and tears, and he goes wholly outside visible things and is separated far from all that is created.

The Spiritual Father as Physician[6]

Just as we send the light of our visible eyes out everywhere and, embracing everything before it by the power of vision, it is not soiled by what is seen—even if that should be exceedingly ugly—but turns unharmed to other things, so is it as well with the reasoning faculty of the saints. Even if it should glance at the swamp of passions and ugliness, it is not soiled. The intellect is naked and alien to every empassioned desire. If such a man were to want to enter into the contemplation of such matters, he would not do so for any other reason than in order to observe and learn the movements and activities of the passions: where they take their origins from, and by what remedies they are in turn dispersed. It is just what we hear of physicians doing, and what we have heard about the ancients. They cut up the dead in order to understand the body's design, so that from those bodies they may learn what the inner parts of living men are, and so try to heal in others those afflictions which are not readily seen. It is, in fact, in something like this manner that the spiritual physician works who, from his experience, wants to heal the sufferings of the soul. But, in order that I may show you in words the art of their treatment, I shall give you a practical example.

Someone ill comes to the spiritual physician. He is stupified by suffering, troubled in all his intellect, and, rather than what heals, he is looking for what is injurious, that is, what gives rise to suffering and brings on death in short order. The physician, loving and compassionate, examines the man, understands the brother's weakness, the passion's inflammation, its burden, and sees that

6 In what follows concerning the "spiritual physician" we again have what is at once a recollection of Symeon the Pious and a traditional image of the spiritual guide.

the one who is sick is quite at the point of death. So who, that I may recall the senseless words of those people, would be seized with desire for a man so ill? In my opinion, one could not infer any such thing against even the most insane of men, on account of the sick man or woman's mortal illness—let alone against pious and God-fearing physicians! But, bidding farewell to the words of people who really are insane, let us return to our example. When the spiritual and knowledgeable physician sees the brother in the condition we have described, he does not immediately argue or shout, or say: "You are asking for something bad and lethal, and I will not give it to you," lest, on hearing this, he take to flight and go off to someone else who has no experience of such afflictions and be dead within the hour. He welcomes him instead, holds on to him, comforts him, shows him at once all affection and simplicity, in order to reassure him that he will undertake his treatment with the same medicines that he has asked for and so fulfill his desires.

You see, there are certain people gravely ill in their souls, and bearing their illness with difficulty, who nevertheless ask for things which aggravate the malady. Now, perhaps the affliction of some of them is such as to require that they diet and abstain from certain foods that please them while they, on the other hand, demand that they be able to take their fill of rich foods to satiety. For this reason, as I have just said, the physician does not immediately agree to what the sick person asks for, but he does promise to fulfill all his requests. The sick man hurries to what pleases him as to something good. The physician disguises what is truly helpful. While the one awaits eagerly and gladly, the other, being wise, shows him what is seemingly like what he desires, but which, hiddenly, is different to the taste and wonderful in the power of its operation. For the ailing one only touches the medications and by that touch alone, beyond hope, receives healing. The burden of his affliction immediately subsides and his wound disappears completely, and those things for which he had previously been enflamed with lust he can now no longer bear even to recall. Thus is it possible to see and behold a miracle occur which is higher than any speech. For without any other help, just by the touch and sight of the healing medication, the physician makes those who are ailing healthy. Their wounds and burdens are reduced, their fiery thirst for those things is quenched. Those who hungered for corrupting and injurious foods from this point on desire instead what is wholesome, and they go on in turn to tell many others about the physician's miracles and the wonderful technique of his science.

Let those who are healthy, if they have received the grace of divine knowledge in fact, listen and understand the meaning of what we have said here in riddles. Those who are ailing do not know these things. Indeed, they do not even understand that they are sick. And who then can ever persuade with argument people thus inclined that they are under the sway of sickness and disease? They imagine rather that it is health to accomplish the wishes of the flesh, and to practise all its lust and desire. And, just as no one will ever make those who are gone mad and deranged take account of the fact that they are insane, just so neither will anyone persuade those who are wallowing in the passions, and ruled by them, and unconscious of their being possessed, that they are in a bad way, and so make them change for the better. For they are blind, and neither do they believe that anyone else can see. Thus they live, deprived of sight and unconvinced they can lift up their eyes. If they were so convinced, then they would look up and, looking up, would clearly see and recognize those who are crucified to the world. Not wishing, though, to be free from the passions, they deliberately plug up their ears and refuse to listen to the Apostle who says:

> The world has been crucified to me, and I to the world [Gal. 6:14].

It is no longer I who live, but Christ Who lives in me [Gal 2:20].

Put to death therefore what is earthly in you: fornication, impurity, evil desire, and covetousness [Col 3:5].

He therefore who has died to the world—for this is the cross—and lives no longer himself, but it is Christ Who lives in him; who has mortified his earthly members, that is, the passionate sensations of the body, such that he has become no longer a participant in any passion or evil lust: how, tell me, can he take in any kind of passionate sensation, or surrender to any movement of pleasure, or ever be troubled in his heart?

Against false "practitioners" and spiritual quacks

If you still doubt and hesitate, just look at whom you are bringing charges against,[7] and at whom it is who you say is a participant in your sin. O, the unmitigated gall! Are you saying that those who have Christ living and dwelling in themselves have lost their heart to sensual pleasure? In that case, according to you, are you saying that Christ is a communicant in sin, Who did no sin, nor was deceit found in His mouth, Who takes away the sins of the world and cleanses the souls of those who are united with Him of every passion? Do you still not understand what we have been saying, but continue to blaspheme it? Do you not shudder, and put your hand over your mouth, and discipline your tongue not to chatter about matters that you have not yet experienced, the knowledge of which your reason has not yet grasped, which you have not seen with your eyes, whose grandeur has not entered into your hearing? Do you not know that they who have had the experience of these things in deed and word laugh at you as at a fool whenever you try to

---

7   The charges in question are likely rumors about the Elder Symeon and as well those which were circulating about—and against—our Symeon himself.

talk about them, and babble on about one thing after another?

If, though, you have been made worthy of the grace from above, then speak freely about what concerns it and theologize without hindrance about Him Who is God by nature. Nor just this, but tell everyone freely about those who are sons of God by adoption, who, so far as it is possible for men, have by grace become like Him in as much as they are holy servants of His glory. But, if you admit that, while doing what is good, you have not partaken of grace, nor felt yourself become dead to the world, nor have known yourself to have ascended up into Heaven so as to be hidden there alone and nowhere else, nor have gone like Paul outside the whole world, whether in the body or without the body, nor have discovered yourself to have been completely changed and, as it were, become spirit by the putting-off of the flesh, and comparing spiritual things with the spiritual, then why do you not embrace the beauty of silence and try, with repentance and tears, to receive and learn these things instead of vainly talking about matters of which you have no true knowledge and wanting to be called a "saint" without having fulfilled these conditions, and carrying on as if you had already been saved while daring to pick up strange notions and teach them to others? Do you not tremble at guiding others to the divine light while remaining yourself deprived of it? Are you not afraid of shepherding others, you who are still sitting in darkness and do not possess that eye which sees the true light? Are you not ashamed to play the physician with others while you are yourself sick and incapable even of taking stock of your own wounds? So, tell me! Unless you have known yourself to be dispassionate and have discovered the dispassionate God dwelling within yourself, what other reason can you have for making so bold, for daring to insinuate yourself into the works of those who are dispassionate, into the ministrations of God's holy servants?

Who dares to presume on the earthly emperor?

See that you do not forget yourself by trespassing on ranks and offices which are strange and alien to you, and so be thrown away into the outer darkness as one who despises the divine will, and as an insolent and useless servant. See that you not be found naked of the senatorial robe and dignity—which, you understand, is nothing other than the grace of the Spirit—and be thus bound hand and foot and cast into the everlasting fire. Watch that you not try to play the shepherd before you have acquired the Good Shepherd as a true friend, since otherwise you will gain nothing other—be sure of it!—than having to give an account to God not only for your own unworthiness, but as well for the lambs whom you will have lost as a result of your inexperience and passions. See to it, I beg you, that you not take on another's debt while still subject to debt in any way yourself, nor dare to grant forgiveness when you do not have Him in your heart Who takes away the sin of the world. See, brother, that you do not set yourself up to judge another before you have become an exacting judge of yourself and an examiner of your own failings, and have loosed the righteous verdict by your tears and compunction. Then truly, filled with the Holy Spirit, in freedom from the law of the flesh and of the death of sin, you will be restored by God's grace as a just judge for the judgement of others as one who is appointed by God for this through the Spirit.

Look, and you will see that no worldly man of importance would dare intrude into this rank before the earthly emperor had enrolled him in the order of judges. And, if there is such order and such fear with respect to human ranks as never to rebel against the earthly emperor, how much more we ought to assign to God's dignity, so as not to be self-ordained and intrude on divine things before being called to them from on high, and thus fall into the hands of the living God. Tremble, man! Honor the long-suffering of God, and do not show less fear for God, the King of Heaven, than worldly authorities have for the earthly emperor. Neither be contemptuous of the wealth of His goodness and long-suffering for the sake of your love for glory and power, because He is Himself the Sovereign of all and the fearful Judge of all Who renders to each according to his works and thoughts. Rather, just as with the earthly sovereign, so should you render honor and fear in turn to the heavenly King and God so that, both honoring and fearing Him, you may be enabled to keep His commandments and, having prepared yourself beforehand by your preserving the commandments, be made worthy of becoming the house of His threefold radiance in accordance with His promises which are no lie. For He says: "He who loves Me will keep My commandments...and I will love him and manifest Myself to him" [Jn 14:21]; and again: "And I and My Father will come and will make our home with him" [Jn 14:23].

Once you have become such a person, you will no longer live for yourself but will see that you have become dead to the world, wearing the flesh as dead and in every case inert with regard to sin, but alive only to God, as moved and energized by Him. And, when you discover yourself in such great glory, you will cry out with a loud voice together with the divine Paul in gladness of heart, and you will say: "I give thanks to my God, because the law of the Spirit of life has set me free from the law of sin and death" [Rom 8:2]. And henceforward you will make no difference between male and female, nor shall you suffer injury because of it, because you will have already received what is natural and will no longer look upon the creatures of God in a manner which is unnatural. Instead, both living and conversing with men and women, and embracing them, you will abide unharmed and be unmoved from the foundation and stability which is according to nature,[8] and will both see and

8   For Symeon, as for the Greek fathers generally, what is fully "natural" in humanity is the state of grace. Athanasius, for example, speaks of St. Anthony emerging from his fortress and

approach them as precious members of Christ and temples of God. Before, however, you have attained to such a measure and behold the life-giving mortification of Jesus, God, at work in your members, you will do well to flee sights which are dangerous. While there is no cause whatever in them for evil, we are still drawn out and enticed into improper lusts by the ancestral sin which makes its home in us.[9]

If you do all this, your whole life will be secured for you, and you will not hit your foot against the rock of sin, whether possessing God already or struggling to possess Him, in Christ Himself our God, to Whom is due all glory, honor, and worship, together with the Father and the Holy Spirit, now and ever, and unto ages of ages. Amen.

---

armed with divine grace as "fully natural (*en toi kata physin*)," i.e., as restored to the condition of Adam before the Fall (*Life of Antony*, *PG* 26.865B). Evil for Symeon, as for the fathers, is precisely the "unnatural (*to para physin*)."

9   The "ancestral sin" (*to propaterikon hamartema*) is not, as in Augustine and the Christian West generally, the guilt of Adam which he passes on in turn through sexual procreation to all of his descendents who, as a result, are all born under the same sentence of damnation passed on the first couple. For Symeon and the Eastern Christian tradition, it is instead the power of evil which was loosed by Adam's sin and so has "infected" the whole creation. It is thus a force, a warping influence, into whose power every human being is born and to which everyone consequently is enslaved. This, at least, is the reading which most of the Greek fathers had of the "sin" and "death" of St. Paul in *Rom* 5:12. Symeon here is therefore advising caution: one should not presume upon dispassion, i.e., freedom from this corrupting force, until such time as he or she truly lives again in grace and cooperation with God, "naturally." See our *Introduction*, Part II, in vol. III, forthcoming.

SEVENTH ETHICAL DISCOURSE

Introduction

Discourse VII, on the true servants of God, sets out to place the ascetic virtues within their proper context. Symeon states specifically that he is addressing himself here to others who are also engaged in the monastic life, the way of repentance. All the tools of asceticism, such as fastings and vigils, struggle for virtue and sorrow for sin, are good and necessary, he declares, but in no way can they be described as doing God any service. They are rather necessary for our own benefit. They alone serve God who do His commandments while we, on the other hand, come to Him as suppliants asking for forgiveness and healing. In a passage which recalls Ezekiel 37, he observes that even the great virtues are merely "dead bones," a corpse, without the fire and light of Christ's Resurrection given in the Holy Spirit. Only thus clothed and illumined, thus quickened, can one be said to be truly alive and in God's service. Therefore, and here he recalls the previous treatise, until such time as we are so clothed we ought humbly to seek the light which is God and meekly accept instruction from those who are truly His servants. There is no place for pride. God will burn up every sin and passion with the flame of His presence. He will make gods of all humanity, as Symeon observes in his closing remarks, though never without the human being's consent. To refuse Him is damnation, while to accept—beginning here below—is everlasting beatitude.

ON THE TRUE SERVANTS OF GOD

The discourse is addressed to monks

Forasmuch as we, without works, reckon ourselves as Christians by virtue of divine baptism, and believe in the consubstantial Trinity and in One of the Trinity, our Lord and God Jesus Christ, and thus style ourselves somehow as simply servants of God, and title ourselves thus while writing to others, inscribing it on the letterhead, and do so perhaps without knowing just what it is that the service of God means, and who it is who is worthy of bearing this title and being a servant of God, I am moved by the Word to exercise my own reason and am urged to speak about those who serve God: who they are, and of what sort, and how, and what the works are which they do for the Lord's sake; since each will know himself from his own works, and whom it is he ministers to by his efforts and whom he serves, or will know whom he has ministered to and served, such that no one rejoicing in serving himself may imagine that he serves the Lord rather than himself. We have, however, nothing to say about those who live in the world and are under the yoke of the present life. St. Paul says explicitly:

> The unmarried man is anxious about the affairs of the Lord, how to please the Lord; but the married man is anxious about worldly affairs, how to please his wife [I Cor 7:32-33]

and the world. Our discourse will thus concern itself exclusively with those who have renounced the world and everything that is in it.

Asceticism is a true service, but only to oneself

Those who have of their own will and by free choice just entered the arena of righteousness and, so far as they are able, exercise themselves in the asceticism of the body, I mean both novices and people who have spent some time in this labor, imagine that they are serving the Lord and hope to be justified by their works. Some of these people, who are inattentive to the light of the holy Scriptures and blinded by the darkness of their own evil reasonings, continually go about outside that light, and so fail to recognize that a great difference exists between those who repent and are struggling with the exercise of virtue, and those who are truly serving the Master, Christ. Sorrowing for the evil things they have done, those who repent ask to receive forgiveness for their faults. Such was the publican, the prostitute, Peter himself, who wept bitterly after he had been frightened into denying the Lord three times, and someone like the prodigal son who squandered his father's inheritance with prostitutes and publicans. These people, and others like them, cannot be said to be serving the Lord. Rather, they are enemies and rebels who seek to be reconciled with Him through repentance and confession. Those, however, who aim at asceticism and who now are bravely training for the exercise of virtue, strive after they have repented to vanquish the passions. They have certainly repented, eagerly and ardently, for their past sins, but it is not for this alone that they struggle now, but as well for the secure possession of the virtues in place of the passions.

The one who is just now repenting grieves, weeps, fasts, keeps vigil, sleeps on the ground, does his service [i.e., in the monastery], and is patient in the face of every trial. He is always thinking of his own evils and holding himself up as worthy of greater punishments. He endures everything which comes to him without being troubled in order that, by such endurance, he may be forgiven his offenses. The good ascetic, however, who is struggling now not so much for the full payment of sins as for the sake of the war against the passions, is prepared for and accomplishes all the above and much else besides. He welcomes every trial which comes to him with joy, and when one does not come, then he afflicts himself. Every work that he hears of which was practiced by the saints of old, or that he sees practiced by his contemporaries, he strives according to his strength to do himself, in order that, by the variety of his ascetic virtues and practices, he may destroy and eliminate completely from his soul the many and varied passions through which the demons exercise their power over us, and so that with all the strength of his soul he may treasure up the virtues in their place. Unless this is what does happen, and if he does not thus possess the fruits of his struggles securely within himself, then he will find no profit in mere estrangement from the passions. For it is not the man who is merely not greedy who is praised, but he who is merciful. Nor is it the man who has kept his talent safe who is saved, but he who has multiplied it; nor is he blessed who simply declines the evil, but he who does what is good. It is not the man who has not allied himself with the King's enemies who is shown love, but the one who takes up arms and does battle against them on His behalf.

The struggle is necessary, but not sufficient

The Master, Christ, also witnesses to this fact when He cries out expressly: "He who is not with Me is against Me, and he who does not gather with Me scatters" [Lk 11:23]. In saying this He shows that the one who does not keep His commandments in every way and with every effort, and who is not constantly acquiring the virtues through the practice of the commandments, is not in fact making any progress, but merely seems to be refraining from evil. Such a man does not cleave greatly to what is good, but has ceased, as it were, from collecting the virtues by virtue of his neglect of the commandments. He cannot even keep what he appears to have, but loses even that because of his laziness; and this is what "he who does not gather, scatters" signifies. Now this is not the case with respect to sensible things, since in that case he who does not gather, but instead sits lazily, is not like someone who scatters. It is different, though, in the realm of the spirit. The divine Scripture regards the one who does not do good as a sinner, and it indicates that he is condemned when it says: "Whoever knows what is right to do, and fails to do it, for him it is sin" [Jas 4:17]; and again: "Cursed is he who does the work of the Lord with slackness" [Jer 48:10]. This certainly suffices first of all for my own condemnation, who am slack and negligent. And if he is cursed who does God's commandments negligently, so much the more greatly will he be condemned who does only a part of what he can do, or who does not do them at all. You will also find that this is the case in civil law and in actual life. The servant who sees his master's house broken into by robbers and his property pillaged, and who neither co-operates with the thieves nor hinders them, nor raises a cry against them, but allows them to make off secretly with everything they have stolen, that servant will probably be considered by his master as an accomplice of the thieves and himself a thief. What then? Would not all of you agree in condemning that servant as a criminal?

This shall certainly be the case for me first of all, who am wretched and lowly—since I hesitate in speaking for all of you, too—if, while refraining from evil works and deeds, I do not hold with all my strength to the virtues in their stead, to such an extent that I become a perfect man and attain "to the measure of the stature of the fulness of Christ" [Eph 4:13], just as Paul requires that we all become. It all makes sense because, if we do not become this, then how shall we have the strength to serve the Lord? How shall we be able to join the army of Christ? And how shall we also arm ourselves spiritually, be mustered in the battle formation of the living God, and show

ourselves as fearful to the enemy? In no way at all! Therefore
let no one imagine that by fasting, or by keeping vigil, or going
hungry or thirsty, or sleeping on the ground, or grieving, or
weeping, or by putting up with the insults and temptations that
assail him, that by such means he is serving God or showing
favor to anyone or anything else. Rather, he is only edifying
himself, and that only if he endures and traverses it all with
humility and spiritual knowledge. If not, then he does not profit
even himself. Whatever does not take place in humility and
spiritual knowledge, whatever it may be, brings no benefit to
the one who does it, and whoever wishes to learn how this is
so will be taught as much by all the divine Scripture. We feel
urged to demonstrate this because neither those in repentance
nor those who have been long in asceticism serve the Lord.
They rather profit themselves, and do good to themselves
alone. Let us now, if you like, support our argument with some
examples.

Example of the emperor's servants: soldiers

Whom do we say are those who serve the earthly emperor?
Are they the people who stay in their own homes, or those who
accompany him everywhere? Are they people who spend their
time in their suburban estates, or those who are enrolled in
military service? Are they people who relax and live luxuri-
ously and riotously at home, or those who show courage and
are wounded in battle, who strike and slay many of the enemy,
and who liberate their fellow servants from captivity and
shame the foe? Are they the goldsmiths and copperers and line
workers who are always at work and barely able to provide for
their own bodily needs and those of their dependents, or are
they the generals, the colonels, the other officers, and the men
whom they lead? Is it not obvious that it is the latter who serve
the earthly emperor rather than the former? Workers in bronze,
and goldsmiths, and artisans, if they do any work for the

emperor, receive the fee agreed upon beforehand from the hands of his subordinates and then, like strangers or aliens, return to their homes without having seen the emperor or being aware of any kind of friendship with him. The generals, on the other hand, and the officers and servants are all known to him. Some, indeed, are the emperor's friends and, through them, so are the men who are under their authority. Now then, imagine with me that this is just the way it is with the heavenly King and those who serve Him. All of us, certainly, believing and unbelieving, slaves and free, rich and poor, priests, high-priests [i.e., bishops], kings and rulers, are His servants in as much as He created and brought us into being. While some, though, keep His commandments gratefully and with all their strength and, giving evidence thus that their faith in Him is sure, are called good and are said to be faithful, others do so carelessly and lazily and, although they do choose to serve Him, are called wicked and troublesome. Others still do or say what is contrary to His ordinances, are His enemies and adversaries, though they are weak and unable to do anything against Him.

But the uniform alone does not make the soldier

We therefore who have heard the Lord say: "If any man would come after Me, let him deny himself and take up his cross and follow Me" [Mt 16:24]; and the Apostle teach: "Children, do not love the world or the things in the world" [I Jn 2:15], "for love of the world is enmity with God," and that "whoever loves the world makes himself an enemy of God" [Jas 4:4], we have put aside the world of appearances and followed our Savior and God. Abandoning the world as for us an impediment to virtue, we have emigrated to the solitary life. It is as if we had abandoned the enemy territory in which we were living as captives after having voluntarily deserted, and have gone back to the country of Christ, our Master and King. We have merely put on the robe of those who are being perfected by

Him, but it is not that we become His servants and soldiers by our [monastic] habit alone, no more than those who wear the same uniform as the emperor's soldiers are for all that necessarily his, or soldiers. Having put on the monastic garb, we do not say that we are His soldiers by virtue of that alone, because our weapons are not bodily but spiritual:

> For our warfare is not against flesh and blood, but against the principalities, against the powers, against the world rulers of the present darkness, against the spiritual hosts of wickedness in the heavenly places. [Eph 6:12]

When, therefore, we are clothed with the armor of light [Rom 13:12], with the shield and helm and the rest that St. Paul has ennumerated [Eph 6:14-17], and have taken in hand the piercing sword of the Spirit, then we can indeed say that we are in His army and have made ourselves ready for the front lines.

While we need asceticism and repentance, God is not served by these

Meanwhile, however, let us see, if you please, what we are to do who have been clothed with the monastic garb and have entered the arena of asceticism and repentance. Do we weep? Why? Of course we do, in order to receive remission of our sins—nor for this alone, but as well that we may be cleansed of the stains which have resulted from sin. Do we fast? Of course, in order to reduce the movements of the flesh and to soften the heart. Do we keep vigil and sing the Psalter? So that we may not think evil things and be turned aside to prideful thoughts. Do we pray bodily? So that we may not be taken captive by the enemy in our minds, and in order to pray always in our intellect, without ceasing. Do we mourn? Certainly, in order to enjoy the joy of compunction. We wear cheap clothing and hair shirts. We sleep on the ground, and many of us bind our bodies with iron chains. Why? In order, of course, to break this lusty body and weigh it down, and not allow it, like some wild donkey unrestrained by any bridle, to drag itself and the intellect which rides it to the edge of the precipice, and over the edge into the abyss of damnation and everlasting fire. So, in doing all this, what good do we provide for those who watch us? Clearly, none whatever. And, if not for those who watch, how much more this must apply to Him Who has given us wisdom and power to save ourselves.

But do we not put up with the mockings and afflictions which come to us with thanksgiving and without rancour? Once again, here, too, we benefit ourselves and not someone else. Listen to the Lord: "If you do not forgive men their trespasses from your hearts, neither will your heavenly Father forgive your trespasses" [Mt 6:15]. So behold, if we should suffer insults, and slaps, and buffetings, and jokes, and spittings, and whatever else, and put up with them gladly, and sympathize from our souls with those who inflict them on us, we benefit ourselves by receiving forgiveness for the sins which we have committed against God. If, on the other hand, we bear a grudge and try in different ways to get our own back for it, we injure ourselves by acting in such a way as to keep our sins unforgiven. Do we sit in a cell, flee to the mountains, dwell in caves, climb up on pillars? Why? Clearly, we are hurrying to escape the one who goes about like a lion and roars dreadful threats against us, and looks for a way to gobble us up. If, therefore, God should grant us help—for without His help we would never escape the fangs of the other and his many fetters, wherever we might flee—and we are saved, and do not become food for that dreadful beast, how can we say that by such deeds we are serving the Lord? This does not seem reasonable to me, nor, I think, to you either.

For how could someone who is being chased by someone else, and is running away from him with all his might, say that

he is serving the man who has delivered him from the enemy
pursuing him by welcoming him into his own house and
closing the door behind him? He could not, but ought instead
to give perpetual thanks to the man who has done him the favor
and delivered him from his enemy. How, tell me, should the
starving who beg for food—whether because they are unwill-
ing to work, or weak and sluggish, or on account of bodily
weakness—be reckoned as serving the people who give them
alms and minister to them? Do not the poor appear rather as the
ones who are being ministered to and freely served by the
alms-givers? So, too, is it that all of us, poor and needy as we
are by reason of our prior iniquities, could never say in our
situation and being what we are that we serve the God Who has
had mercy on us. We are all, as we said, whether by reason of
prior sins, whether from evil habits, whether from lassitude and
sloth regarding God's commandments, or from the deliberate
choice of evil, or from a preference for sensual pleasures, or
from ignorance and disbelief in the divine Scriptures, or again
from conceit and imagining that we need nothing more for the
salvation of our souls: all of us, simply put, are poor and naked.
Nor is this all, but, because we are also wounded, possessed by
many kinds of disease, dying wretchedly, or even somehow
walking about in our cells and monasteries as people do in
hospitals or nursing homes, we cry out and lament and weep,
and we beg Him Who is the physician of souls and bodies (as
many of us, that is, as have awakened to an awareness of the
pain of our wounds, that is, of the passions, since there are
indeed people among us who, like some folk of "sound mind,"
do not know that they are sick at all, or possessed of any
passion) that He come and heal our wounded hearts, and grant
health to our souls which lie prostrate on the bed of sin and
death, because, according to the divine Apostle [Rom 3:23], all
of us have sinned and we all require His mercy and grace.

The ascetic virtues are "dead bones" without the Holy Spirit

Being what we are, do we therefore dare to say to Him Who has had mercy and compassion on us, Who heals our souls and teaches us what is necessary for salvation, and Who, after a little while, provides us with the healing of our wounds and diseases, that we in any way serve Him? Of course not! Neither was the man who was wounded by the thieves and left lying half-dead said to have served him who put him on his own beast and brought him to the inn, and who applied wine and oil to his wounds. To the contrary, he was shown mercy, and healed, and brought back to his original health by the other [cf. Lk 10:30-35]. Consequently, given that we are weak and maimed and wounded, and heedless of hastening to do anything for our own healing, as I have said, how shall we dare or even conceive that we are serving the Lord? In no way can we do so. What then? If we are at all aware of our condition, as I just said, we beg and pray for the healing of our diseases. When this happens, and when, from the top down, we put off the illness little by little like a garment grown old and torn and soiled, and put on health like a shining double cloak from the crown of the head to the tips of the toes, then we, too, ministering to others with wine and oil and with the rest of the dressings and medications, may reckon ourselves as serving the same Lord Who said: "As you did it to one of the least of these, My brothers, you did it to Me" [Mt 25:40]. If, however, we are not first in this condition, but try to do these things while we are still sick, the Master will answer and say to us: "Physician, heal yourself" [Lk 4:23].

You heard us call the health of the soul a shining cloak. Do not laugh at the expression out of ignorance, nor suppose that we are talking about bodily health instead of about something which is bodiless, and divine, and of the intellect, something which does not derive from medications and herbs, "Nor be-

cause of works, lest any man should boast" [Eph 2:9]. Just as
someone is not profited at all by putting dead bones together
with dead bones, and joints to joints (you might take this image
and apply it to works and the possession of virtue), since he
lacks the ability to complete the project by weaving them
together with flesh and nerves. And, even if you were able to
complete the work, and join the joints to the nerves and clothe
those dead bones with flesh, and assemble the whole into a
body, still there will be no profit. It lacks the spirit which gives
life and animates it; that is, it is deprived of a soul. Please
understand that the same applies regarding the soul which is
dead. Turn your mind to what is within the soul's members,
and consider that all its actions taken together—I mean fasting
and vigil, sleeping on the ground and a hard bed, non-possession and abstinence from bathing, and everything which follows from these—are like dead bones fastened to one another
and all consequent one upon the other, and that, assembled
together, they comprise as it were the complete body of the
soul. So where is the profit if it lies unsouled and breathless,
the Holy Spirit not being within? For only when the Latter
comes and makes a home in us does He then come and bind
together with nerves of spiritual might the acts of virtue which
were dead and, like souless limbs, lying scattered from each
other, and unite them to the love of God, and so reveal us as
new who were old, and as alive who were dead.[1] There is no
other possible way for the soul to live.

As our body, whether ill or not, is unable to move or even
live at all without a soul, so our soul, too, whether it sins or not,

[1]   This passage is based on Ezk 37, the prophecy of the "dry
      bones" and resurrection of Israel. In the present office of the
      Byzantine rite (perhaps in Symeon's time, too?), this text is
      appointed for the matins of Saturday in Holy Week. Again, the
      individual Christian stands in here for the Church, the "Israel
      of God."

is dead without the Holy Spirit and can in no way live everlastingly. If sin is death's sting, clearly he who has sinned has been stung and is dead; and, if no one is without sin—for everyone, Paul says, has sinned and been deprived of God's glory [Rom 3:23]—then, obviously, all we who have sinned have died and are dead. So imagine yourself together with me as spiritually dead. Then tell me how you may truly live without having been united with the true life, that is, the Holy Spirit, through Whom every believer is regenerated and made alive again in Christ? "I am the truth," He says, "and the resurrection, and the life" [Jn 14:16 and 11:25]. The servants and disciples of Christ are light and truth and life. "He who receives you," He says, "receives Me, and he Who receives Me receives Him Who sent Me" [Mt 10:40]. If we are dead and He alone is life everlasting, let us not say that we serve Him before we have been united with Him and live. How can the dead ever serve anyone? Unless we put Him on consciously, like a cloak, let us not think that we have been freed at all from our infirmities and the passions which trouble us.

The Holy Spirit is food and drink and clothing

Just as the darkness does not go away unless the light is present, so the disease of the soul is not banished unless He Who takes away our infirmities comes and unites Himself with us. He is called health when He comes because He chases away every disease and infirmity of the soul and gives us back our health; and He is called light, Who transcends all light, because He illumines us; and life, Who is beyond all life, because He vivifies us. Shining around us all, and encircling and cherishing us with the glory of His divinity, He is called raiment, and so we say that we clothe ourselves with Him Who is intangible in every way and Who cannot be grasped. Uniting Himself without mingling with our soul, and making it all as light, He is said to indwell us and, uncircumscribed, become circum-

scribed. O the miracle! It is thus that He Who transcends all
things is said to become all things for us: bread, shelter, and the
water of which He said to the Samaritan woman of old that he
who would drink of it would never thirst. So, if you are still
thirsty, you have not yet drunk of that water, for He Who said
this does not lie. I once heard someone[2] say: "From the time
the Master Who loves mankind gave me to drink of this water
to satiety, if it ever happened that I forgot and, as one who had
not drunk, asked again that He give me to drink, that same
water which I had drunk before would leap within my heart and
spring up like a stream in the form of light, and I would see it
immediately. Pulsing within me, it would speak in a way and
say to me: 'Do you not see that I am with you inside? And
where would you ask that I be given you, or where else should
I appear? Do you not know that I am always with those to
whom I have given Myself once for all to drink of Me, and that
I become in them a spring which does not die?'"

Therefore seek only Him, humbly and without pretentions

Therefore, brother, if you know this to have taken place
also in yourself, you are blessed. And if you have seen Christ,
but He has not yet given you this drink to drink, prostrate
yourself, weep, entreat, lament, strike your own face like
Adam once did, pluck out the hairs of your head. Do not lie
down on a bed, but let your bed be the ground. Do not give
sleep to eyes, nor rest at all to your eyelids [Ps 132:4]. Do not

2   Symeon is probably speaking of himself here, although his
    words echo Ephrem the Syrian's two hymns on the Samaritan
    women. See Kathleen E. McVey, trans. *Ephrem the Syrian:
    Hymns* (New York: Paulist Press, 1989) 354-364. The clothing
    imagery also supports Ephrem's influence. See Sebastian
    Brock, "Clothing Metaphors as a Means of Theological Ex-
    pression in Syriac Tradition," in *Typus, Symbol, Allegorie bei
    den ostlichen Vätern und ihre Parallelen im Mittelalter*, eds.
    M. Schmidt with C. F. Geyer (Regensburg: 1982) 11-40.

turn your glance aside to anything on earth or in heaven—for what is anything else to you who see the Creator of all before your eyes? Never fill your stomach with food. Do not sweeten your throat with delicacies or drink to satiety. Do not be curious about things which are happening [around you], nor look aside to those who live in indifferent and contemptible ways, lest you fall into conceit or, worse, condemn them. Neither should you ever sit down to untimely conversation with them. Nor should you circulate in search of famous monks, nor inquire into their lives. Rather, if by God's grace you have chanced on a spiritual father, tell only him about yourself. If not, but as seeing Christ, look always at Him and in all things keep Him alone as the One Who sees your sorrow and affliction.

Show Him, indeed, let Him see your lack of washing, your extreme want of possessions, your refusal of money. Neither if all the wealth of the world were to flow at your feet or a great heap of gold were to be cast before you—for such things happen by the evil one's machinations, and by those of his co-workers and champions—would you want to turn your eye at all and look away to them, even if the poor seemed to give you an excuse to take and distribute it. Let Him see you struck and not returning the blow, insulted and not replying in kind, reviled and blessing those who revile you, not looking for glory, nor honor, nor rest, but simply doing and accomplishing all things without flagging in any way or turning backwards, until He have compassion on you and grant that you drink that fearful and ineffable and unnameable drink. And, when you have been made worthy of this, you will know what we are talking and have been telling you about. "For," says the Apostle, "we are speaking wisdom, not of this present age which is passing away, but we impart a secret and hidden wisdom of God" [I Cor 2:6-7].

But if you have not been deemed worthy of seeing Christ Himself at all, how can you imagine that you are alive? Why do you think that you are serving Him, Whom you have never seen? Having neither seen Him nor been made worthy of hearing His voice, how will you be taught His holy and well-pleasing and perfect will? And if you say that you will learn it from the holy Scriptures, I will ask: "How, since you are dead and lying in darkness, will you be able to hear or to fulfill it in order that you be made worthy of living it and of seeing God?" You never will! So what then? If the Apostle says that we are dead and dwell in darkness, how shall we have the strength to live, and how shall we see Christ, the true Light Who has come on the earth? Listen carefully and do not try to justify yourself, but humble yourself before God and say: "Lord, Who desire not the death of a sinner, but that he turn and live; Who came down to earth for this reason, that You might raise up those who were lying slain by sin and make them worthy to see— so far as it is possible for man to see—You, the true Light; send me a man who knows You so that, by serving and obeying him with all my strength as I would You, and by doing his will as I would Yours, I may be well-pleasing to You, the only God, and may be deemed worthy, even I a sinner, of Your Kingdom."

Not everyone serves the emperor directly—they are also blessed who serve his friends[3]

If, then, you thus persist with all your strength and soul,

---

3   A very important qualification. Not everyone is given to see God in this life, and Symeon—despite his usual emphasis—will on occasion acknowledge this. After all, this, too, is an undoubted fact of experience. Everyone, however, is without exception required to pray for this grace. Note as well that in what follows the believer, if not accorded the vision, is obliged to listen to and obey those who are, "God's friends"—a note St. Gregory Palamas will repeat in the *Hagioretic Tome* (cf. PG 150.1228C-1229B). In the following paragraph we find again the note of defensiveness regarding the slanderers of the Elder Symeon: they are those "who do not wish to serve officers who are spiritual."

knocking, begging, and asking Him, He will not abandon you but, whether through Himself or through one of His servants, He will teach you as many things as you need to do and, through His grace and the prayers of His servant, will grant you the strength to accomplish them. For without Him you will be able to do nothing. He, though, as I have just said, will be all things to you unceasingly. And if He does not become all things, at least you will be found to be seeking Christ at the hour of your death, at least you will be found subject to His friends and authorities and serving Him through them—for the will of God is the will of His servants—at least you will be found working and not idle, in humility and not in conceit. Remember what I have said: the generals and officers are, on the one hand, all servants, but, on the other, they are also the friends of the King, and, through them, so are the people who are directed by each of them. The latter, even if they do not see and meet the emperor, but serve their general or officer as well as they would the emperor himself, hope to receive through their leaders gifts and decorations from the king. And, indeed, they do receive them, putting forward as intermediaries their officers. There are others, too, who by virtue of their own courage and virtue become famous, and who are received and honored by the king, and established in turn as rulers and intermediaries for others, and then are deemed worthy of doing their service in the presence of the king himself, and converse with him, and hear his voice.

If, however, as was said before, you do not persist in seeking and knocking, but come under anonymous soldiers, that is, prefer to be enrolled as a paltry subordinate to paltry men, and do not wish to serve officers who are spiritual, why do you blame me for calling you dead, or blind, or infirm and weak, and far away from the service of Christ the King? But perhaps you will say that you sit in your cell attending to yourself, and do no one any harm in any way? Would you, then, accept that your servant or cell attendant should do the same, so that, by holding your service in contempt and going off to sit in another cell, he would not be doing you or anyone else an injustice? Would anyone stand for hearing such an idea? How then do you claim to be serving God by sitting in your cell and being attended to by others? Tell me, by what deeds? Even if you were to minister to yourself in every respect, and were to have what was necessary to your body by virtue of the work of your own hands, even so you could not say that you were serving God. No servant is praised for feeding and clothing himself. On the contrary, unless he supplies his own lord daily with what is commonly called the tribute, he is condemned and punished as useless. So how then do we, living as free men and giving ourselves up to comfort and slackness and indolence, and who not only neither work nor serve others, but also grow annoyed, and blaspheme, and grumble by the hour unless someone else is ministering to us, how can we say that we are serving God and doing no one an injustice? As many people as one is able to serve while not choosing to do so, so many does he wrong, and he renders himself liable to judgement and to the Master's verdict, which says as follows:

> Depart from Me, you cursed, into the everlasting fire prepared for the devil and his angels; for I was hungry . . . [and He goes on to list what follows, concluding:] I was sick, and you did not minister to Me [Mt 25:41-43].

So how, and with what kind of face, shall we look on Him when He comes to examine the works of each?

Aflame with God, the soul can truly see its sins

Make no mistake! God is a fire, and has come as fire, and has cast fire on the earth. The same Fire goes about looking for kindling to seize upon, for a ready disposition and will, in order to fall upon it and ignite it. And in those in whom it is kindled, it rises up into a great flame and reaches to the heavens, and it allows the one so enflamed neither delay nor rest. Neither, as some people imagine about the dead, does it consume the burning soul unawares—for the soul is not lifeless matter—but with perception and knowledge and, in the beginning, with unbearable pain, since the soul is both feeling and rational. Afterwards, when it has completely cleansed us of the filth of the passions, it becomes food and drink, light and joy without ceasing within us, and, by participation, it makes us light ourselves. It is like a clay pot that has been set on the fire. At first it is somewhat blackened by the smoke of the burning fuel, but after the fuel has begun to burn fiercely, then it becomes all translucent and like the fire itself, and the smoke can communicate none of its blackness to it. Just so, indeed, does the soul which has begun to burn with divine longing see first of all the murk of the passions within it, billowing out like smoke in the fire of the Holy Spirit. It sees in itself as in a mirror the blackness which accompanies the smoke, and it laments. It senses its evil thoughts like thorns, and its preconceptions, being consumed like dry kindling by the fire and reduced completely to ashes. After these things have been utterly destroyed and the essence alone of the soul remains, quite without passion, then the divine and immaterial fire unites itself essentially to the soul, too, and the latter is immediately kindled and becomes transparent, and shares in it like the clay pot does in the visible fire. So, too, with the body. It, too, becomes fire through participation in the divine and ineffable light.

Concluding Exhortation

This will never come to pass in us, however, unless we abominate the world and everything in it, and unless, in accordance with the Lord's saying, we lose our own souls. That fire is kindled in us in no other way. Those who have received it have not only been completely delivered from all the maladies of the soul, but have also healed many others who were ailing and infirm in spirit, snatching them out of the devil's claws and bringing them as gifts to the Master, Christ. These people, having been wisely instructed in every science and every art by that divine fire, were in every respect and in their whole way of life, and throughout their lives, well-pleasing to God. Such was Peter, the divine Apostle, who received the keys of the Kingdom; such was Paul, who was taken up to the third heaven; and so in succession were all the divine Apostles. So, too, were our holy and God-bearing fathers and teachers, who by this divine fire made the heresies disappear, who subdued the demons like useless and infirm slaves (and the latter, obeying them with fear, became just that and will always remain so), who loved God so much as not to spare their own souls. These holy ones, and as many as are like them, are therefore said to have served and to serve God forever, but those who are still subject to sins are not. They are instead likened to wicked servants and rebels against their Master. Those still troubled by passions are like people continually at war, like people who are wrestling with or resisting enemies. Those who have not yet acquired the virtues, but are struggling to possess them, are like people whose bodies have been mutilated, or like the poor who lack the necessities of life, who need the limbs and requirements which they lack and who cannot thus provide others with what they need, nor are able to serve without wages.

According to the Apostle's word, we are forthwith required to acquire every virtue in order to accomplish the perfect man according to God, that is, the man who lacks nothing in any way, and to receive the grace of the Spirit from the heavenly King like soldiers taking their rations from the earthly emperor. And then, when we have become already perfect men, and have risen up to the maturity of Christ and its measure, and have been enrolled with His soldiers and servants, we shall campaign against our hostile enemies since, as Paul the divine Apostle says, no one "ever serves as a soldier at his own expense" [I Cor 9:7]. What does "expense" mean? The royal ration. If, therefore, we should not also receive from God the bread which comes down from heaven and gives life to the world, that is, the grace of the Spirit—for this is the spiritual ration by which they are nourished who campaign with Christ, and with which they are spiritually clothed in place of weapons—then how, tell me, shall we march with God's army? How shall we be ranked among His servants?

So come, let us rise up, as many of us as wish to escape the slavery of the passions, and run to Christ, the true Master, so that we may acquire the title of His servants. Let us also strive to become such men as our discourse has just ennumerated. Let us not, therefore, hold our salvation in contempt, nor fool ourselves and make excuses for our sins by saying: "It is impossible for a man of the present generation ever to become such a person." Neither let us philosophize against our own salvation, nor argue against our very souls. Because it is indeed possible, if we will it so, and so much so that free will alone can carry us up to that height. For where, as St. Basil says,[4] there is a ready will, there is nothing to hinder. God wills to make us gods from men, but only with our consent and not involuntarily. So do we then withdraw, shaking off His beneficence? How great a foolishness, madness and ultimate stupidity, would this not be? So much does God wish this that, coming forth without departing from the bosom of the blessed Father, He descended and came down for this reason to the earth. Thus if we, too, should wish it, there is nothing that can hinder us in any way. Only, let us set out by way of ardent

4 In *S. Bap.*, *PG* 31.437B.

repentance to Him, and He, having drawn nigh to us and having touched our hearts with His spotless finger, will kindle the lamps of our souls, and will never suffer them to be quenched unto the consummation of the age, for eternity and beyond, because to Him is due all glory, honor, and worship now, and for ages of ages without end. Amen.

EIGHTH ETHICAL DISCOURSE

Introduction

Discourse VIII is something of an interlude, with none of the echo of controversy which runs through the treatises surrounding it. Symeon does, however, elaborate on themes present in the preceding treatises. Christ comes to save, and His salvation does not come from our works. We are called first and foremost to love Him in faith. Meditating on His mighty works, the soul is softened and warmed. Love then takes shape within the soul as a pearl takes form within an oyster. The pearl, though, is not of us but of heaven, of the Trinity, and it takes up its place within the soul as light whose joy surpasses every earthly thing. There is nothing to compare with the indwelling love of God, and the latter is given us freely (*dorean*) in faith. None of our works amount to anything whatever in comparison with it. All the tools of asceticism are, literally, nothing (*ouden*). God looks for faith in a humble and contrite heart, and only to such a heart will He come and make His home, disperse the passions, and fill it instead with the fruits of the Spirit and the revelation of the "abyss of the hidden mysteries of Christ." Therefore, the first and fundamental necessity for the Christian is to cultivate repentance, tears, and purity of heart.

ON THE LOVE OF GOD AND FAITH

What the Son of God endured for our salvation

Let us listen, if you please, to God our Savior Who cries out expressly to us and says: "I have not come to condemn the world, but that the world might be saved through Me" [Jn 3:17]. And, wishing to show us the way of salvation, He says: "God sent His Son into the world, that whoever believes in Him should not perish but have eternal life" [3:16]. Whoever therefore believes these things from his heart and is assured that Christ came not to judge but to save him, and not by his own labor or effort or sweat, but by faith alone in Him: how, tell me, should he not then love Him with all his soul and all his mind? And this especially when he hears all that He suffered Who wills to save both him and all humanity: His descent from heaven; His entry and conception in the womb of the Virgin and Theotokos; how He became man Who is above the heavens, of equal honor and co-essential with the Father, and rules all creation with the hand of His power, Who is on high with the Father and deigned to become an infant here-below in accordance with the sequence of our nature.

And, together with these, when he takes into account the remaining mysteries of His Incarnation, nor this alone, but as well what sufferings He Who is by nature without suffering endured for his sake, such as: His inexpressible birth, the swaddling clothes, the cave, the manger of dumb animals in which the King of all was miserably laid, the flight into Egypt, the return from Egypt, the reception by Symeon, how He was blessed like a common human being by the latter and introduced into the Temple; His submission to His parents, the baptism by John in the Jordan, the temptation by the devil, His miracles and on their account not being admired but rather envied and insulted and ridiculed by all (and by whom? by evil and godless men whose open mouths He could visibly or invisibly have stopped up, could have dried up their tongues and quenched their voices within them); the betrayal of the disciple; the binding by the murderers which He endured; how he was led by them as an evil-doer and betrayed to Pilate as one condemned, and received blows from a slave, and silently accepted the verdict of death (for Pilate says: "You will not speak to me? Do you not know I have the power to release you and power to crucify you?" [Jn 19:10]); then the scourging, the mockeries, the curses, the purple robe, the reed, from which He accepted the blows of the God-slayers upon His immaculate head, the crown of thorns which He wore Who weighs all things in the balance; and, to put it simply, when he considers how He was led out of the city to the place of the skull, the populace and soldiers surrounding Him together with an innumerable crowd drawn to the spectacle; and, in addition to this, angels shuddering on high, and God the Father seeing His co-essential, co-honored, and co-enthroned Son suffering these things from the impious Jews, and being hung naked on the Cross and fastened to it with nails in His hands and feet, His side pierced by the spear, and given vinegar with gall to drink, and enduring all things not only with long-suffering but praying on behalf of His crucifiers—how will he not love Him with all his soul?

When he remembers that [although He was] God without beginning from a Father without beginning, of one nature and co-essential with the all-Holy and adored Spirit, invisible and unsearchable, He came down, was incarnate and became man, and suffered all that we have said and many other things for his sake, so that He might set him free from sin and corruption, and make him a son of God and a god like Himself: well then, even if he were harder than rock and colder than ice, would not his soul be softened and his heart warmed toward love of God? For my part, I say and confess it to be true that if a man believes all these things from his heart and from the depths of his soul, he will also and immediately have the love of God in his heart.

The pearl of great price: God's love and light, the Trinity

Imagine that the love of God is sown in us in just the same way as they say that the pearl in the open shell is conceived by the dew of heaven and the lightning. When the soul hears of the sufferings of Christ just recounted and little by little believes in them, it opens up in proportion to its faith where, before, it had been closed by unbelief. And, when it has been opened, the love of God, like a kind of heavenly dew which is joined with an ineffable light, falls immaterially on the heart in the guise of lightning and takes the form of a shining pearl. Concerning this pearl, our Lord says that when the merchant had found it, he went off and sold all his belongings and bought it. So, too, he who has been deemed worthy of believing in the way we have said, and of finding the intelligible pearl of the love of God in himself, does not stop at merely despising all things and distributing all his belongings to the poor, but allows those who wish even to pillage them in order that he may keep his love for God inviolate and wholly undiminished. The latter, growing daily in the heart of him who prefers it to everything else, becomes in him a miracle of miracles, both inexpressible in every way and in all respects indescribable, neither grasped by the mind nor uttered in words. Ecstatic at the inexpressibility and incomprehensibility of the thing, and fixing his intellect in meditation upon it, the man goes wholly outside of the world—not in his body, but—in all his perceptions, for the latter also withdraw together with the intellect to what is contemplated within him.

Thus, too, the man in this state begins to observe what he is seeing, and looks and, behold, there is light; and the light seems to him to have its origin from on high. He then looks and finds that this light, being perfect, possesses neither beginning nor middle. And, while he is puzzling over these matters, behold, there are Three in the light: the One through Whom, the One within Whom, and the One in Whom. And, when he has seen Them, he asks to learn about Them, and then hears distinctly: "Behold, I am the Spirit, through Whom and in Whom is the Son;" and: "Behold, I am the Son, in Whom is the Father." While he becomes yet more puzzled, the Father speaks in His turn: "Behold, you see." "And I," says the Son, "am within the Father." And the Spirit is saying: "It is truly I, for he who sees through Me, sees the Father and the Son, and is transported by the seeing beyond the things which are seen." Where are They Whom he sees? "There, where no one knows among men, nor among angels, save My unique oneness and essence which transcends essence and nature." He says "in Me." How? "All at once together, for I am inseparable and indivisible in every way, preserving the One even in the Persons. If then you are somewhere or somehow in Me, you would not know in which of Us you were. While you, who are circumscribed in as much as you are a man, I become as it were circumscribed and in a place—for One of Us indeed became a mortal and circumscribed—yet, according to the nature which is Mine, I am altogether invisible, uncircumscribed, formless, intangible, impalpable, immoveable, ever-moving, filling all things while altogether nowhere at all, not in you, not in any of the angels or prophets who have approached Me of old or who now draw near, by whom I have never been seen at all, nor am seen now."[1]

He who thus beholds these things mystically and is initiated into what is beyond angels, beyond human comprehension,

1 The monk's conversation with the Holy Trinity recalls *Catechesis* 36.224-254; English: deC, 375.

will such a man be at all able to be with other men either in perception or in intellect? For if someone were ever to be found worthy to be presented to and converse with the mortal emperor, and were to forget eveyone else in order to hang entirely on the emperor's words, then how much the more would someone deemed worthy of seeing (so far as it is possible for a man to see) the Creator and Master and Lord of all, "Whom no man has seen nor ever can see" [I Tim 6:16], and conversing with Him, and listening to the voice of Him Who is going to judge the living and the dead, not be transported out of himself and, truly, go outside the world and the flesh, and yearn to be with Him? But, on being separated from so good and great a thing—something transcending everything good and great—would he then come back to the cares of this life and trouble himself at all over things which are corruptible, and passing, and ephemeral? There is no way, I think, that a man of sound mind would ever admit that someone so graced could return to that.

Faith and humility attract God's mercy

While it is acknowledged that good things in the present life have sadness, despondancy, and pain as their accompaniment and consequence, yet the life and converse with God, and the contemplation of His unspeakable good things, go beyond all beatitude and transcend every glory, prosperity, joy, and ease. They are exalted above the honor and delight and enjoyment of everything which is supposed to be good in the present life. As much as dying on a soft and sumptuous couch is preferable to being laid on a burning grill, so much does the joy and rejoicing which comes to the soul in union and converse with God transcend every festivity and enjoyment of this life. For this reason, then, even the man who has often separated himself from the better things due to laziness or ignorance, and has turned to the concerns of this world, to the degree that he senses the bitterness and unbearable hurt that is in them, he comes running back to those things which he had left, much blaming himself that he had been dragged down completely and had entered among the thorns of this life and the fire which burns men's souls. He flees then, and runs back to his own Master, and, unless the Latter were not a lover of mankind and did not receive us who return to Him and did remember our evil or become angry with us instead of accepting our return to Him, no soul even of a saint would have been saved, even if it were in some intermediate condition or other. For this reason, all who have been perfected in sanctity and virtue were saved by grace, and not by works of righteousness. Nor just these, but all who afterwards are being made perfect will also be saved in the same way.

Since according the divine Apostle it is "Not because of works, lest any man should boast" [Eph 3:9] that salvation comes to us who believe, we must not be confident at all in our works—I mean fasting and vigils, sleeping on the ground, hunger and thirst, binding the body with irons or troubling it with hair shirts. These things are nothing at all, because many indeed among the evil-doers and the wretched have endured such things and remained the same, neither ceasing from their evil nor improving from their wickedness. While these actions do contribute a little to dragging the body down toward humility, or better, to incapacity and infirmity, yet this by itself is not what God is seeking. He longs instead for a broken spirit, a humbled and contrite heart, and for us always to speak our heart to Him with humility: "Who am I, my Master and God, that You came down and took flesh and died for me, so that You could deliver me from death and corruption, and make me a communicant and participant of Your glory and divinity?" When, according to the invisible movements of your heart, you find yourself in this state, you will discover Him immediately embracing you and kissing you mystically, and bestowing on you a right spirit in your inward parts, a spirit of freedom and of remission of your sins. Nor this alone but, crowning you as well with His gifts, He will make you glorious with wisdom and knowledge.

What else is so dear to God and welcome as a contrite and humble heart, and pride laid low in a spirit of humility? It is in such a condition of soul that God Himself comes to dwell and make His rest, and that every machination of the devil remains ineffective. All the corrupting passions of sin vanish completely. The fruit of the Holy Spirit alone weighs heavy in the soul, that fruit which is love, joy, peace, kindness, goodness, faith, meekness, humility, all-embracing continence, followed in succession and beauty by divine knowledge, the wisdom of the Word, and the abyss of Christ's hidden counsels and mysteries. He who has arrived at becoming and being endowed with these qualities is changed for the good, and from a man he becomes an angel. In the body here-below he circulates among men, but in his spirit he lives and converses with the angels, and in joy inexpressible stretches himself out to the love of God. To that love no one among men has ever drawn near unless first he purified his heart through repentance and many tears, and penetrated the depths of humility, and became pregnant with the Holy Spirit, by the grace and love for mankind of our Lord Jesus Christ, with Whom be glory, honor, and majesty to the Father together with the Holy Spirit, now and ever, and unto ages of ages. Amen.

NINTH ETHICAL DISCOURSE

Introduction

Discourse IX takes up again the thread of controversy. Here
Symeon writes against bookish theology and those who pro-
mote it. All human knowledge, he declares, is inadequate to the
mystery of God. Not even the letter of Scripture or the writings
of the fathers reveal the depths of the Trinity. The latter can be
known only in faith, and in souls whose perceptions have been
purified. All the more reprehensible, then, are those people
who, themselves still caught up in the passions, presume to
knowledge of the God Who is without passion and, worse yet,
who have the unmitigated gall to slander the saints who do
know Him and in Him are made new. Symeon is clearly
alluding earlier in these passages to his elder, Symeon the
Pious. Later on he makes the reference explicit, citing his own
experience of the light of the Spirit which he received at the
prayers of his spiritual father. He goes on to describe the marks
of sanctity. The saints are known by the vesture of divinity
which clothes them and indwells them. Those who are not pure
in heart, on the other hand, are caught in the snares of the devil.
Their iniquity is evident in their skepticism regarding God's
saints whose virtue and experience they deny. To the accusation
of his adversaries that he is himself presuming on privileges
accorded to the Apostles alone, Symeon replies that such as SS
Paul and John were themselves sinners at one time and that our
calling, together with the *charismata* that accompany it, is no
different in essence than theirs. Each Christian is therefore to
strive to know his or her own sins, to seek contrition and

humility, and then and only then will he or she recognize the
saints by virtue of the same Holy Spirit Who is the source of
all true knowledge and virtue in God.

THAT TRUE KNOWLEDGE COMES FROM PURITY AND
THE GRACE FROM ON HIGH

The Holy Spirit, and not human learning, leads to the knowledge of God

Now is a good time to say with David, and say it the more
loudly: "The Lord looks down from heaven upon the sons of
men to see if there is any who is wise, that seeks after good"
[Ps 14:2]; then: "They have all gone astray, and become useless; there is not one that does good, no not one" [v. 3]. "Where
then," that I may add the words of the Apostle to the foregoing,
"is the wise man? Where is the scribe? Where is the debater of
this world? Has not God made foolish the wisdom of the world"
[I Cor1:20] such that, by means of it, one is able to know the
true wisdom, the God Who truly is? Brothers, if the full
knowledge of the true wisdom and the knowledge of God were
going to be given to us through letters and formal study, what
need would there be then for faith, or for divine Baptism, or
even communion in the mysteries? Obviously, none whatever:

> For since, in the wisdom of God, the world did not know
> God through wisdom, it pleased God through the folly
> of what we preach to save those who believe [I Cor
> 1:21].

This is what the herald of the Church says, the man who leads
her to her Bridegroom, Christ.

For my part, I will naturally grieve and weep at the break-
ing up of my own members, my own race, of brothers according to flesh and spirit, because we who have put on Christ

through baptism account the mysteries of Christ as nothing. We think we will receive the full knowledge of God's truth by means of worldly wisdom, and fancy that this mere reading of the God-inspired writings of the saints is to comprehend Orthodoxy, and that this is an exact and certain knowledge of the Holy Trinity. Nor is this all, but the more august among us foolishly suppose that the contemplation which comes to pass only through the Spirit in those who are worthy is the same as the thoughts produced by their own reasoning. How ridiculous! How callous! Indeed, these people, who have plunged sacrilegiously into the depths of God and hurry on to do theology, when they hear of God that in the Trinity there is the light of a single godhead just as there is a single mingling of light among three suns, right away picture three suns in their imagination, united in the light which is the essence and distinguished in the hypostases, and then stupidly imagine that they see the divinity itself, and that the holy, consubstantial, and undivided Trinity is just like their imagined paradigm.[1] But it is just not so, not at all! For no one is able to think or speak properly about what concerns the holy Trinity from just reading the Scriptures. One instead accepts it by faith alone, abides with what has been written, and does not dabble with anything more. As for those who are curious and dare to meddle cheerfully with divine things, [they should understand that] it is not possible to say anything at all outside of what has been written and taught by the fathers.

Listen to what Christ says in confirmation:

No one knows the Son except the Father, and no one knows the Father except the Son and anyone to whom the Son chooses to reveal Him [Mt 11:27].

1   The image of the "three suns" for the Trinity is taken from Gregory of Nazianzus' *Vth Theological Oration*, see *Introduction*,Part II, in vol. III, forthcoming.

With these and similar sayings He therefore shuts up the shameless and flapping mouths of those people who say and think that by exterior wisdom[2] and book-learning they know the whole truth, know God Himself, and possess knowledge of the mysteries hidden in God's Spirit. For if no one knows the Son except the Father, neither does anyone know the Father except the Son and whomever the Son may wish to reveal the Former's depths and mysteries to. In effect, He says that "My mystery is for Me and My own". Who then among men on earth, wise men, or rhetoreticians, or mathematicians, or others, save those who have cleansed their intellect by the supreme philosophy and asceticism, who thus bring to the task a soul whose perceptions have been thoroughly stripped, could ever know the hidden mysteries of God from merely human wisdom and without the revelation which comes through the Lord from on high? These are mysteries which are unveiled through an intelligible contemplation enacted by the operation of the Holy Spirit in those to whom it has been given—and is ever given—to know them by virtue of the grace from on high. Knowledge of these things is for them whose intellect is illumined daily by the Holy Spirit on account of their purity of soul, whose eyes have been clearly opened by the rays of the Sun of righteousness, whose word of knowledge and word of wisdom is through the Spirit alone, whose understanding and fear of God, through love and peace, are preserved firmly in faith by

---

2   The "outer wisdom (*he exo sophia*)" refers to secular learning, in particular the Greek philosophers (especially Plato). It is distinct from the "inner wisdom" given in the Holy Spirit. Symeon is giving expression here to the tension between Byzantine humanists and, especially, the monks, a tension which had been long in place and which would enjoy its last important battle in the fourteenth-century confrontation between Gregory Palamas and his opponents—see D.M. Nicol, *Church and Society,* 31-65.

the sanctity and goodness of their way of life. Of such people is the knowledge of divine things, and to them, as to the Apostles whom they imitate, Christ says: "To you it has been given to know the mysteries of God, but for others they are in parables" [Lk 8:10].

The saints who know the Trinity are slandered by people who only think they know

These are therefore the ones who, moved by the divine Spirit, know the equality of honor and union of the Son with the Father. For they behold the Son in the Father and the Father in the Son through the Spirit, as it is written: "I am in the Father and the Father in Me" [Jn 14:11], the Spirit being clearly with the Father. For if the Spirit proceeds from the Father, and the whole Father is in the whole Son, the whole Holy Spirit is also in Both. Father, Son, and Holy Spirit are one God, He Who is worshipped by everything that breathes. And how will you be able to say that three suns are one? Since, if you do unite them, they will become one and the three only one. If not, then you have sinned against the Unity. But you will never find the Father without the Son and Spirit, neither the Son without the Father and Spirit, nor the Spirit a stranger to union with Him from Whom He proceeds. The Father and Son are in the Spirit, and in the Son there is the Father with the Spirit, and the Son is and abides co-everlastingly in the Father and has the Holy Spirit shining forth together with Himself. Believe it! These are one God and not three. In three hypostases is He Who is, and is eternally, and is ever the same, praised on high by innumerable powers in a single oneness of nature and kingdom and divinity. While the traits common to the divine identity are seen in each of the Three, nonetheless these Three are One and Each is the One—which is not possible in the case of suns.

I would have liked to provide some image which would have presented clearly the meaning of what I have just said for those who make bold to know, by means of their so-called "knowledge" alone and without the Spirit Who searches the depths and the mysteries of God, but I reverence the God Who said not to give holy things to the shameless and presumptuous, nor to cast pearls before people who think about the divine as they would about the profane, and who, as it were, dishonor and trample them underfoot with their grubby notions and ravening souls. As the prophet says [cf. Is 6:9-10], God has blinded their intellect and hardened their heart, so that seeing they see not, and hearing do not understand. And rightly so, because they have made themselves unworthy by their conceit and evil practices. This is why they have been allowed by God to walk in the darkness of their own unbelief and wickedness, as David says: "So I gave them over to their hearts' perversity, to follow in their evil ways" [Ps 81:12]. They have the great examples of the fulfillment of God's commandments which our fathers have perfected in their works and have set before us who believe for the faithful imitation of virtue, yet they wanted neither to understand nor to imitate them. Quite the contrary, in fact, they derided them and slandered the lives of those who had struggled to live in accordance with God by saying they were not in accord with Him. How are they unworthy not only of divine knowledge but, as sons of rebellion and damnation, worthy as well of every punishment and condemnation? Because, as it were, they forget to examine themselves closely to see whether or not they are within the faith, they judge what is none of their business, and foolishly examine and question matters that are beyond them. They have no shame before the God Who says: "Judge not, that you be not judged" [Mt 7:1]; and: "With the judgement you pronounce you will be judged" [Mt 7:2]. Nor have they any excuse before His disciple, who says: O man, "who are you to judge the servant of another. It is before his own master that he stands or falls" [Rom 14:4];

and: "Judge not one another, do not speak evil against one another" [cf. Jas 4:11-12].

How, then, can such people be known as believers and Christians, who thwart the sayings of Christ and His Apostles and do not keep them as He and His disciples enjoined, nor follow and walk in the Teacher's footsteps? How shall they who openly transgress the divine commandments ever see the light of those commandments? They will not! Brothers, he says, "Let no one deceive you with empty words" [Eph 5:6]. And Paul calls us brothers by virtue of the spiritual regeneration and kinship which is from divine baptism since, as I see it, we have made ourselves aliens by our works to the brotherhood of the saints. I will try to demonstrate this from the facts themselves; or rather, it will be our own deeds and words which shall reprove us. In order to make this clear I shall continue my argument from this point on as if addressing an audience of one.

The gall of those who presume on God and wrong the saints!

Have you, O brother, renounced the world and what is in the world? Have you become one who possesses nothing, and submissive, and a stranger to your own will? Have you acquired meekness and become humble? Have you fasted to the supreme degree, and prayed, and kept vigil? Have you acquired perfect love for God, and have you regarded your neighbor as yourself? Do you intercede with tears for those who hate and wrong you, and are hostile to you, and do you pray they may be forgiven those offences, having first had compassion on them from your soul? Or have you not yet been led up to this height of the virtues? Tell me! If you are ashamed of saying "no", or else do not want to say "yes" for the sake of humility, I shall myself, brother, set the facts before you and will show you right now from what sort of deeds and accom-

plishments everyone who struggles with genuine understanding and sanctity arrives at this summit of virtue. Therefore
if, as we said just now, you have arrived at all that was said
before and have loved your enemies, and have often wept tears
from your heart for their sake, have besought their entire
conversion and repentance, then it is clear that you have
achieved all the rest. You have become in some fashion dispassionate as a result of your struggles. You have acquired a heart
cleansed of the passions, and in and through it you have seen
the God Who is without passion. For it is not possible otherwise to pray lovingly out of a compassionate heart for one's
enemies, unless, by our co-operation with the Good Spirit and
our contact and unity and contemplation of God, we have come
into the possession of ourselves as pure of every stain of flesh
and spirit.

So if, brother, by the grace of God Who has saved you, you
have arrived at this condition with kindness and humility, why
do you disbelieve them who have struggled and been led to
these things together with you, and envy them, and slander
them with reproaches, and try to drag down their good name?
Do you not know that those from the first hour who were
jealous of those who had arrived around the eleventh, because
the latter received the same wages, were on that account
thrown out into the outer fire? And how do you, who do the
same and worse, and who speak against the saints whose lives,
virtues and understanding shine like the sun, how do you think
you will not be subjected to the same torments or, indeed, to an
even worse punishment? Or do you not know there is no envy
among the saints, since it is written: "Where there is envy, there
abides the devil, the father of envy, and not the God of love."[3]
Plagued by envy, how do you fancy yourselves as holy at all,
you who are not recognized as either a believer or a Christian

3   I do not know whom Symeon is quoting here.

for the sake of your love of God and of neighbor? It is obvious to everyone who listens to the divine Scripture that this is the case, and that he who suffers from envy has the devil within himself and cannot be said to be of Christ because he has no love for his neighbor.

If you have not yet been deemed worthy of such great gifts, nor have attained to so great a height of the deifying virtues, how then do you dare at all even to open your mouth and speak? How, being still a catechumen, do you decide to teach, and try to meddle in matters about which you neither know nor have heard, and then, as if you knew about divine things, proceed to argue boldly about such matters? Do you not know that, as a sort of catechumen, your place is outside the Church doors and that even if you persuade yourself by presumptuous self-opinion that you have a place with everyone who is praying faithfully and truly, you are not following the Apostolic Canons?[4] By catechumen here I do not just mean the unbeliever, but as well the one who cannot reflect the glory of the Lord with the uncovered countenance of his intellect [cf. II Cor 3:18]. For my part, I greatly lament your folly because, while both then and now you completely fail to believe that a great man is a saint,[5] at the same time, while counting yourself as a common man among common men, you speak as if you were some kind of saint and a God-bearing man inspired by the Holy Spirit. Stung by my argument, what you say you know nothing about and admit that you have neither seen, nor heard, nor been found worthy of receiving in your heart, these things you have no shame in interpreting and clarifying as if you did know, nor do you blush at men's laughter. So, if you are not become dispas-

4 Const. Apos. 34.11
5 Again, and in the following paragraphs, Symeon is referring here to his elder, Symeon the Pious—"our holy father"—though once more without naming him.

sionate, as we have said, nor worthy of having the Holy Spirit, nor are a saint, how can you say you know, as if you were a saint, the things of the Holy Spirit concerning which it is written:

> No eye has seen, nor ear heard, nor the heart of earthly man conceived, the good things which God has prepared for those who love Him [I Cor 2:9]?

Symeon's testimony to the revelation of the Spirit at the prayers of his Elder: One lamp kindles another

As for us though—that I may speak like a fool since you force me to it—who are least and wretched, in accordance with His unspeakable goodness towards us and at the intercessions of our blessed and holy father, God has through His Spirit revealed for us to know what the Apostle calls "the gifts bestowed on us by God" [I Cor 2:12]. "For," he says, "the Spirit searches even the depths of God" and "We have received not the spirit of the world, but the Spirit which is from God" [I Cor 2:10 and 12]. Through him [i.e., Symeon the Pious] the God and Father of our Lord and Savior Jesus Christ, the great God, was revealed and made known to us, lowly sinner that we are, in Christ God Himself, Whom no man has seen nor can see. The same Who said: "Let light shine out of darkness, He it is Who has shone also in our hearts" [II Cor 4:6], worthless and good for nothing though we be. He is encompassed like a treasure by the earthen vessel of our tabernacle, the Same Who is in every respect both incomprehensible and uncircumscribed. Without form or shape He takes form in us who are small, He Who fills all things uncircumscribably and transcends both grandeur and plenitude.

This taking form in us of the Good Who truly is, what is it if not surely to change and re-shape us, and transform us into the image of His divinity? We know that the holy Symeon the Pious, he who was a monk in the monastery of Studion, became such a one, and we have been confirmed in this by experience itself. For having had our faith in him confirmed by the revelation of the Spirit within him, we hold this truth as incontestable. Yet more: the lamp of our own soul was kindled by communication from his light, as flame from one lamp to another. We preserve [that flame] unquenched, are guarded by his prayers and intercessions, whence our faith in him is watered and grows, and—I speak with boldness before God—will grow yet more in the divine light until it bears fruit a hundredfold. For the holy light without evening is a fruit of faith, and the holy light in turn an addition and growth of faith, since as much as the light springs up, so much does faith grow and ascend to the heights. And, according to the measure of faith, the fruit of the Spirit ripens visibly: "But the fruit of the Spirit is love, joy, patience, kindness, goodness, faithfulness, meekness, self-control" [Gal 5:22]. The man who possesses them knows each of these virtues. Just as the owner of sparkling stones, sapphires, amethysts, and other such, knows (unless he is inexperienced) the form and size of each of them, so, too, does he who with toil and tears has planted the virtues in himself and has harvested the fruits of the Spirit know both the form and the quality of each of them, and tastes of all their sweetness, and what is greater and more marvelous, he recognizes that same fruit in others.

Who is a saint? One who keeps the commandments

Just as we recognize the different nations by their clothing and most people by their voice and speech, just so then do we recognize the saints by, on the one hand, their decency and attractive behavior and other outward signs; but it is their speech, on the other hand, which truly and accurately reveals their real identity. What the heart does not have, the mouth is unable to produce. If such a person should then speak, he is immediately reproved as speaking badly by his words themselves. For the Lord says: "The good man out of the good treasure of his heart brings forth good, and the evil man out of the evil treasure of his heart brings forth evil" [Mt 12:35]. Now, let us consider the depths of the spirit here, how the Lord did not say only that "from his good heart he brings forth good," but added "from the treasure of his heart" in order for you to learn that none of us can have a dumb and empty heart. Either each person possesses through good works and true faith the grace of the Spirit, or else, because of faithlessness and inattention to the commandments and accomplishment of evil, he carries around in himself the wicked devil. That you not think that He means they have the treasure of the Spirit who only keep His commandments in part, and in part despise them, but that it is only for those who keep them all, He makes it clear by saying:

> He who has My commandments and keeps them, he it is
> who loves Me; and he who loves Me will be loved by
> My Father, and I will love him and manifest Myself to
> him... and I and my Father will come to him and make
> Our home with him [Jn 14:21-23].

Whoever does not keep them gives entry to the devil

Do you see how he who has acquired a good heart through his efforts and by doing the commandments has acquired the whole Godhead, which is that good treasure, to dwell within him? That such a great treasure does not abide in the man who transgresses a single commandment, no matter which, or who neglects and fails to accomplish any of them, listen to our Lord once more:

> Whoever then relaxes one of the least of these com-
> mandments, and teaches men so, shall be called least in
> the Kingdom of Heaven [Mt 5:19].

He calls those commandments "least" not because they are such, but because we reckon them to be so. For by our thinking

lightly of idle talking, or of lusting after something belonging
to our neighbor, or looking at something with passion, or
despising and insulting someone, we become indifferent and
forget Him Who has placed all these actions under judgement.
So, what does He say about them? "On the day of judgement
men will render account for every careless word they utter" [Mt
12:36], and elsewhere: "You shall not covet anything of your
neighbor's" [cf. Ex 20:17]; and again: "Anyone who looks at
a woman lustfully has already committed adultery in his heart"
[Mt 5:28]; and:

> Whoever insults his brother shall be liable to the coun-
> cil, and whoever says 'you fool!' shall be liable to the
> hell of fire [Mt 5:22].

When, too, the Apostle wishes to show that the devil is at work
in those who do such things, he says: "The sting of death is sin"
[I Cor 15:56]. Therefore, if sin is nothing other than transgression of a commandment, and if it is a commandment not to lie,
not to covet, not to steal, not to talk idly, not to speak harshly
to one's brother, then everyone who does any of these things
has been pricked by the sting of death which is sin, and into the
wound left by the bite of sin the devil, like a worm, slips in
immediately and is found to dwell.

Have you seen how those who have not yet acquired their
own hearts purified through tears and repentance have the devil
indwelling them, the devil who is the evil treasure? Thus does
the good man bring forth good from the good treasure of his
heart, and the evil man in like manner evil. True repentance
through confession and tears, like a kind of medicine and
dressing, cleanses and clears away the wound of the heart and
the scar which the sting of spiritual death had opened in it.
Next, it casts out and puts to death the worm which had nestled
there, and restores the wound to complete healing and perfect
health. This activity is found only in those whose hearts are

seeking diligently, with tears and repentance, for health. As for the rest, they actually take pleasure in these wounds. Nor is that all, but they are eager in fact to scratch them and add still other wounds to them, thinking that health is the satisfaction of their passions. Thus they indeed boast whenever they accomplish some wicked indecency of sin, and count their shame a glory. Why do they endure this? Because they are ignorant of the sweetness and joy of complete purity, or rather, they do not believe in it and have persuaded themselves that it is impossible for a man to be perfectly purified of the passions and receive the Comforter in himself wholly and substantially.

Symeon's opponents prove their perversity by not recognizing the saints

For this reason, therefore, they are always talking and acting against their own salvation, both locking the gates of the Kingdom of Heaven against themselves and hindering anyone else who might wish from entering. If, indeed, they hear of someone else who has struggled lawfully with the Lord's commandments and has become humble in his heart and thoughts, that he is purified from every kind of passion and is proclaiming to all the mighty acts of God—that is, as many things as God has done for him in accordance with His unfailing promises and how, for one, speaking for the edification of his hearers, he was made worthy of seeing the light of God and God in the light of glory, and, for another, how he knows consciously in himself of the visitation and operation of the Holy Spirit, and has become himself holy in the Holy Spirit—then immediately, like ravening dogs, they bark at him and try if possible to gobble up the man who says such things. "Stop!" they say, "you deluded and prideful man! Who in our time has become such as the holy fathers became? Who then ever saw God or ever could see any part of Him? Who ever received the Holy Spirit to such a degree that he was made worthy of seeing through Him the Father and the Son? Stop! lest we stone you to death with rocks!"

I do not think it necessary to reply to them in a manner worthy of their foolishness. The wise Solomon says:

> Answer not a fool according to his folly,
> lest you be like him yourself.
> But answer a fool against his folly,
> lest he be wise in his own eyes [Prov 26:4-5].

Among such as you, as you say yourselves, no one has ever seen God in any way. But among those who have chosen to take up the cross and travel the narrow way and lose their own souls for the sake of everlasting life, many indeed have seen of old and even more, I think, see now, and each of those who wish it will see Him, even if you, by reason of your paltry malice and perverted thought, are unable to pick them out. Now, see what the evangelist says:

> As many as received Him...to them He gave power to become children of God; who were born, not of blood, nor of the will of the flesh nor of the will of man, but of God [Jn 1:12-13].

If you yourself have not been born of God, it is therefore clear that you are not His child, nor have you received Him nor taken Him into yourself. On account of this, He has neither given you power nor are you capable of becoming a child of God. Not having become God's child, how then will you be able to see God, your Father in heaven? No one has ever seen his father before being born, and no man will see God unless he has first been born of Him. For this reason the Lord also said: "Unless one is born from above, he cannot enter the Kingdom of Heaven" [Jn 3:3]. You then, if you are born only from the flesh and have not yet known the birth which is from the Spirit, how can you search the depths of God? How can you see God? Obviously, not at all. You yourself, brother, will admit this, albeit unwillingly.

So be it! What then? "But you," says my interlocutor," are you such a one yourself? And how shall we recognize that you are such?" While I myself, without the grace from on high, am not such a man as could say this, neither, I think, was Paul himself, nor John. Yet I groan at the hardness of heart of those who put forward these excuses to me, and who ask how they might recognize the man who has arrived at perfect humanity, at the full measure of the stature of Jesus. If you want to learn, it is how the blind recognize other men, how Isaac knew Jacob while the latter was clothed with the vesture of his brother, Esau. All of you know how puzzled he was, saying: "The hands are the hands of Esau, but the voice is Jacob's voice" [Gen 27:22]. Here it is shown that while he could not penetrate the deceit of the clothing, he was blind after all, still he knew the usual voice of his son. Therefore, if he had also been deaf, he certainly would not have been able to recognize Jacob's speech. This is then the case with you, too, who are puzzled in a similar way, but who happen not only to be blind, but deaf as well. How are you able to know a spiritual man? Not at all, certainly. That it is true that those who do not see spiritually cannot hear spiritually either, listen to the Lord as He is speaking to the unbelievers among the Jews: "Why do you not understand what I say? It is because you are unable to hear My words" [Jn 8:43]; and a little later He says:

He who is of God hears the words of God; the reason why you do not hear them is that you are not of God [Jn 8:47]

...You are of your father, the devil, and your will is to do your father's desires [Jn 8:44].

If then you are also fleshly because of unbelief and wickedness, because of neglect and transgression of the commandments, I say that you have fattened your heart and have stopped up its ears, and that the eye of your soul has been veiled by the passions. How in that case would you be able to recognize a spiritual and holy man?

There is no ascent to the heights of God without the depths of humility

My fathers and brothers, I beg you instead that we strive in every way for each of us to know himself, in order that from what is our own we may learn what is beyond us. For it is impossible for a man who has not recognized himself beforehand so as to be able to say with David: "But I am a worm and no man" [Ps 22:6]; or again with Abraham: "I am but dust and ashes" [Gen 18:27], to understand any of the divine and spiritual Scripture in a spiritual way, in a fashion worthy of the wise Spirit. Let none of you be deceived by empty and specious arguments that anyone can at all comprehend the divine mysteries of our faith without the Spirit Who initiates us into the mysteries and illumines us. Nor can anyone become even a receptacle of the Spirit's charismata without meekness and humility. It is incontestably necessary for us first of all to lay the foundation of faith securely in the depths of our souls, then through the manifold forms of virtue to erect inward piety as a kind of fortress wall, and then, the soul having been walled all around and virtue, as it were, planted within it as on a solid foundation, then indeed one must raise the roof of this edifice, the roof which is the divine knowledge of God, and so complete the whole house of the Spirit.

When a man's soul has been purified by tears, and in proportion to his repentance and fulfillment of the commandments, he is first deemed worthy of knowing by grace what is proper to him and his entire self. Then, after much intense purification and profound humility, he begins little by little to perceive in some obscure way things which concern God and the divine, and, to the degree that he perceives, he is wounded to the quick and acquires yet greater humility, deeming himself entirely unworthy of the knowledge and revelation of such mysteries. Thus, too, guarded by such humility as by a fortress wall, he abides within it unwounded by presumptuous thoughts, and grows daily in faith, in hope, and in love for God, beholding clearly his progress with the increase of his knowledge and of his ascent. When he attains to a full measure of the maturity of the fulness of the knowledge of Christ, then he will conduct himself as one who neither has nor knows anything, and will consider himself as a useless and unworthy servant. And, what is then astonishing and beyond nature—or, better, is quite according to nature—he will think that there is no man in all the world lesser or more a sinner than himself.

As for the "how," I have nothing to say, unless it is the following alone which I have been able to grasp about this praiseworthy state. The soul, being made such and its thought immersed by the Spirit in the depths of that humility which is in Christ, has forgotten the whole world and everything in it. It regards ever only itself and what pertains to it, and, having been long in this study and having entered wholly into this condition, it sees itself as truly nothing and most vile, and is convinced there is no other so wretched among all the men in the world. Thus, as much as one sees oneself in his own soul's perception as more wretched and lowly than all men, to just such an extent will he also be first among all others, as our Lord and God says: "If anyone would be first, he must be last of all and servant of all" [Lk 9:35].

O brothers, let us therefore also strive to attain to such a degree and condition, and let us readily recognize the saints who have attained to it, and so we shall also obtain the present and future good things, by the grace and love for mankind of our Lord and God and Savior Jesus Christ, to Whom be glory and majesty, now and ever, and unto ages of ages. Amen.

ELEVENTH ETHICAL DISCOURSE

Introduction

Discourse XI, on the "Life-giving mortification of Christ in the perfect," advances the thought which concludes the preceding discourse. The form of this world is passing away and the Christian is called to die to it by putting on the virtues. In an extended metaphor, Symeon compares the body and soul of the believer to the palace and treasury of the emperor. The King Himself, God, encounters us in the depths of our soul. Our lives are in quest of this meeting and the virtues stages on its way. Symeon then returns to the theme of Christ as "en-personed love (*enhypostatos agape*)," the supreme virtue and font of virtues. The glory of God in Christ dwells within us when we commune with and know this love. At the same time, every impassioned thought or sinful deed will cause Him to desert His dwelling place within us (literally, in our breasts, *enstethios*). But, if we chase away every passion, then He is "suddenly (*aiphnes*)" found within revealing to us the "whole spiritual universe." The discourse's second half is devoted to the dangers of assuming pastoral office within the Christian community. Such a charge is to be avoided at all costs, and accepted only in obedience to God's voice urging one to do so—and then only with reluctance and sorrow. Symeon repeats the dire condemnation of Israel's shepherds in Ezekiel 34, and concludes with an exhortation for each to remember that Christ is to be served alone and that, in doing so, each Christian is to seek first the shepherding of her or his own soul, the acquisition of dispassion, and the light of the Spirit. Then and then alone may one presume to serve the servants of God.

ON THE LIFE-GIVING DEATH OF JESUS GOD WHICH
OCCURS IN THE PERFECT

Even if some imagine they do, still, not everyone who hears of
the Lord Jesus discerns the effects of His life-giving death and
its miraculous activity which is ever bringing virtue and knowledge into being in the perfect, but only those who have recognized and clearly understood that most holy saying of the
Apostle which goes as follows:

> The form of this world is passing away, [so] let those
> who have wives live as though they had none, and those
> who mourn as though they were not mourning, and
> those who rejoice as though they were not rejoicing, and
> those who buy as though they had no goods [I Cor 7:31,
> 29-30];

so, too, those who have cares as though they had no cares, and
those who work as though they were not working. And again
he says: "As dying, and behold we live...as having nothing, and
yet possessing everything" [II Cor 6:9-10]. Therefore, do not
simply hurry past these words and think that you have somehow
thus understood the power which is hidden in them, but instead
examine precisely with me, beloved, the interior condition of
your soul, and we shall present you with an illustration drawn
from the visible world of what was said above. Pay careful
attention to what we say!

The mansions of the righteous and palace of the King are
to be entered in sequence and purchased with blood

He who is already dead is not disposed to the perception of
anything visible, and he who has nothing has been deprived of
everything. He is in need of all. He longs for everything. On
the other hand, there is the man who has everything. Toward
what other thing in this life might he direct his desire who

obviously possesses it all and lacks for nothing? What, indeed, should he want to possess? But blessed is he who in his deeds has sought the things mentioned, and has seized and learned and seen them by experience! For our words are not empty words. Rather, just as houses and cities and kingdoms are arranged according to location by streets and regions, so too, in the path which leads up to heaven, the commandments of God and the virtues are laid out according to degrees and locales. We therefore speak about these matters to the degree which speech permits in order to bring to light the magnitude and beauty of these invisible creations. As for the man who reads about them, however, how can he arrive at seeing them from the words alone? In no way, you might say. And if he is unable to visualize them, how might he become master of them? It is certainly possible to do so partially, or to see something of them in part, but it is not possible to possess them. For while everyone finds it quick and easy to repeat what he has heard to others, to possess any of these is to purchase it with a price. What is given for the purchase of such things is not gold nor silver, but blood, because everyone of us who wants these things buys them one by one with his blood. Truly, unless one is slaughtered like a sheep for any single virtue and pours out his own blood for it, he will never possess it. God has so ordered it that we receive eternal life by means of our voluntary death. Do you want to die? You do not? In that case, you are dead already.

Now let us look at the mansions and houses of the virtues, what and of what sort they are, for the sake of whose acquisition one is obliged to empty his blood. The first house is blessed humility, because He says first: "Blessed are the poor in spirit, for theirs is the Kingdom of heaven" [Mt 5:3]. The man who wants to enter this house and acquire together with it the Kingdom of heaven, unless he is first bound hand and foot before its gates like a sacrificial ram and gives himself up to slaughter to anyone who wishes, and is immolated and dies

completely through having slain his own will, shall never enter
within, nor of a certainty will he ever possess it. And if he does
not acquire this virtue, then neither will he obtain any of the
others. Because it is impossible for anyone who skips over this
stage ever to arrive at the next since God has arranged for
everything to be in order and by degrees. Indeed, just as islands
in the deeps of the sea, so should you picture with your mind the
virtues to be in the midst of this life. They stand apart from one
another and are linked, as it were, by certain bridges which are
removed and suspended far from all things earthly, and they
bind the one virtue securely to the others. The beginning of all
of these is blessed humility. A man enters it via the western gate
of repentance and, after sojourning there a sufficient time,
departs via the eastern gate and crosses the bridge to come thus
to the abode and dwelling place of mourning. There, too, he
abides for a time until, having been both washed and cleansed,
and after having been nourished by its beauty, he passes on to
the hostel of meekness, and from there he comes running to the
place of hunger and thirst for righteousness, and then he discovers the palace of mercy and compassion. Then, when he has
gone beyond the last, or rather has entered within it, he comes
to the royal vaults of purity, and on going inside sees enthroned
within the King of Glory, He Who is invisible to all creation.

Conceive with me of the body as the palace and the royal
treasury as the soul of each one of us. God has joined Himself
to it by the doing of the commandments and He makes it all full
of divine light, makes it indeed God, by virtue of His union
with it and His grace. Everyone comes to this state of adequacy
to God who traverses the path of the virtues which we have just
described, but it is altogether impossible to happen along by
any other direction and to jump over this or that mansion in
order to arrive at the next by some kind of trickery. It is thus
that the Master, Christ, has arranged that the entry to the

Kingdom of heaven should occur, and it is impossible that it should happen in any other way. For if the sea cannot surpass its bounds, just by that much shall these limits be preserved unbroken and unchanged. To take another comparison, the ascent of those who hurry toward heaven is like a ladder and its steps. While each of us is to be more zealous in climbing up the ladder's steps than the other so as to catch up with our neighbor, it is altogether impossible and beyond human power to avoid beginning at the bottom and going up step by step, and instead somehow by-pass the first rungs in order to get to the higher ones. Those who do walk outside this direct path and sequence greatly fool themselves. Just as it is never possible to climb up into an elevated house without a ladder, or to enter the royal chamber itself where the emperor lives without passing through the forecourts of the palace, so is it impossible for the man who does not place his feet according to the order described to enter into the Kingdom of heaven. Everyone who goes outside the royal highway—let no one mislead you—walks unaware of his having gone astray.

A prayer for Christ's assistance and thanks for His mercies

But, O Lord, guide of those gone astray, the unerring path of those who come to You, turn us all around and place us before Your ladder, and direct our hands with Your own hand to take hold of it, and enable us to raise ourselves from the earth and to step onto the first rung, so that we may know that we have somehow, sometime, taken hold of something with our hands and have raised ourselves a little from the earth. For we are obliged to ascend, just a little, at first to You, in order that You, the good Master, may come down from so far away and unite Yourself to us. Show us, Master, the door at the forecourt of Your Kingdom, so that we may knock patiently at it until the gate should open to us by virtue of our voluntary death, and we enter within and knock one by one at the gates and open them. May You Yourself, hearing our groans and the beating of our breasts, hurry to come down from Your high chambers, You the greatly compassionate and merciful God, that we may hear the sounds of Your all-immaculate feet and know that You are opening the innermost gates, closed to sinners, and drawing near us and saying: "Who is he who is knocking?" and that, answering with cries and tears, we may reply to You with trembling and joy: "We are, Master, we the unworthy, the wretched, Your cast-off and wicked servants, we who until now have been wandering astray among mountains and cliffs and ravines. We are those who have senselessly soiled Your holy Baptism, who denied our covenants with You. We are those who have fled away and even deserted voluntarily to Your enemy who plots against our souls. Now, though, having remembered You and Your love for mankind, we have run away from there and, weary with labor, have come to You in great fear and trembling.

"Forgive and be not angry with us, Master, but with mercy and compassion for us wretched ones open to us, Lord, and do not call to mind our evils, neither bear rancour for our ingratitude, for we have stood long hours in knocking, nor misunderstand us, Your servants, lest, having been slighted, we turn backwards. We have grown weary beating on the doors to the forecourts of Your Kingdom. Open to us, You Who by nature love mankind, have compassion on us. For if only You open to us the door of Your mercy by a little, who will not shudder at seeing You? Who will not fall prostrate in fear and trembling and beseech Your mercy? Who, seeing You Who have ten thousand times ten thousand angels and a thousand thousand archangels, and thrones and powers, abandoning the heights and coming down to us, and meeting and opening to us, and both welcoming us graciously and falling upon our necks and kissing us, who will not be immediately wounded to the quick and undone as if he were dead? And his bones will be poured out on the earth like water, and he will weep day and night reckoning up the ocean of Your compassion and goodness, and reflecting the glory and splendor of Your countenance. Glory be to You Who have arranged things thus. Glory to You, Who have been well-pleased to be seen by and united with us. Glory to You, Who for the sake of Your great compassion are revealed to and seen by us, You Who by nature are invisible even to the heavenly powers themselves. Glory to You, Whose mercy toward us is unspeakable, Who have deigned through repentance both to abide and to walk with us."

Christ: the treasure within Who asks for silence and permits no rival

O grandeur of ineffable glory! O excess of love! He Who embraces all things makes His home within a mortal corruptible man, He by Whose indwelling might all things are governed, and the man becomes as a woman heavy with child. O astonishing miracle and incomprehensible deeds and mysteries of the incomprehensible God! A man carries God consciously within himself as light, carries Him Who has brought all things into being and created them, including the one who carries Him now. He carries Him within as a treasure inexpressible, unspeakable, without quality, quantity, or form, immaterial, shapeless, yet with form in beauty inexplicable, altogether simple, like light, Him Who transcends all light. And, clenching his hands at his sides, this man walks in our midst and is ignored by everyone who surrounds him. Who can then adquately explain the joy of such a man? Will he not be more blessed and more glorious than any emperor? Than whom, or than how many visible worlds, will he not be more wealthy? And in what shall such a man ever be lacking? Truly, in no way shall he lack any of God's good things.

But be watchful, that I may address you directly, you who have been deemed worthy of becoming such a man as to possess God entire dwelling within you, lest you ever do or say anything unworthy of His will and, by His leaving you, immediately lose the treasure hidden within you. Honor Him to the best of your power, and introduce nothing into His house which is displeasing to Him or which offends His nature, lest He permit it and then go away angry with you. Do not use many words with Him, nor prostrate yourself while calculating shamelessly to yourself and saying: "I will show Him excessive ardor and a great zeal of love, so that He may accept my intention and know that I love and honor Him." Know therefore that, before you even conceived these thoughts, He knows all your rationalizations before anything has been said. But neither should you try to seize Him with the hands of your intellect, for He is ungraspable, and the more you make bold to touch Him or fancy that you hold Him, the more you will have nothing inside and He will immediately disappear from you entirely. Then you will greatly regret it, and will weep and beat and whip yourself, and it will do you no good whatever because, since He is joy, He does not accept entry into a house of sorrow and grief, just like the busy bee will not go into a house full of smoke. If, however, you have prepared yourself with joy and without anxiety, He will be found once more inside you. Therefore allow the Master to take His rest untroubled upon the couch of your soul.

And do not begin again to say within yourself that, "Unless I weep before Him, He will turn me away as one who despises Him." While you were still repenting before and approaching perfection He wanted you to weep, and would at times allow you to glimpse Him and at times be hidden and at still others shine on you, and He did this to provide for the purification and ornamentation of the house of your soul. After repentance and cleansing through tears, however, He appeared in order to provide you with rest from your labors and groans, and with joy and cheer in place of grief. So stand up, and I do not mean merely with the uprightness of the body, but in the motions of your soul and its impulsions. Be silent. The King of kings comes to your home. I tell you, speak vigorously to all the doorkeepers of your house: "The King is coming! Stand at attention at the doors! Stand in silence and with much fear! Let no one come knocking at the door! Let no one's shouting enter within from near or far! Let no one enter secretly, lest the King abandon us immediately and be gone again!" Therefore, when you have said these things, stand in rejoicing and gladness of soul. See your uncircumscribed Master circumscribed within you still uncircumscribed, and know unknowably His all-holy face, and learn His inconceivable beauty which is, indeed, unapproachable to angels and archangels and all the heavenly powers. Be astounded, rejoice, and leap with joy and gladness in your spirit, and attend with patience to whatever He may command you to do or say.

Pay attention then to what I am telling you. He is not like the earthly kings, in need Himself of His subordinates to ask after something for His own service and needs, for He is without need and, unless He first makes His own servants wealthy, does not enter into their homes. He is without need, as we said, and when He has made you wealthy and without need by means of His own wealth, pay attention to what He says within you Who has come down from so great a height, from heaven, and come forth without separation from the blessed bosom of the Father even to your own lowliness. You will never find that He has done this off-handedly. Rather, our good and beneficent Master has ever been used to do this for the salvation of many others as well. Therefore if, as we said, you honor and accept Him, and give Him a place and provide

Him with silence, know well that you will hear ineffable things from the treasuries of the Spirit. You will not be falling on the Master's breast, as did John the beloved of Christ beforetime, but you will carry the Word of God entire within your breast. You will declare theologies both old and new, and will know well all the theologies which have been written or spoken already; and you will become an instrument the Artist plays to make sounds pleasing beyond all music.

If, on the other hand, you allow sorrow coming from somewhere to peep into your house, joy will straightaway fly away; and if wrath or anger, He Who is meek and calm will immediately give way; and if hatred and disgust against anyone, He Who is called love—and is such truly by His own nature and in His very Person—will immediately depart. If you allow envy or strife to draw near, He Who is good and carries no grudges, abominating these things, will vanish entirely. And if He knows that wickedness and trickery together with idle curiosity are carrying-on outside the house and you do not quickly chase them away with anger, but He sees you treating meekly with His enemies and allowing them to get near Him, neither will He Who is simple and without evil or meddling let you know of His departure, but will simply abandon you as one who is without feeling. You, who have been deemed worthy of meeting such a Master, who have become a beholder of such glory, who have entered into the possession of such wealth—I mean the wealth of the Kingdom of heaven which is God Himself—take care that none of the things mentioned enter the house of your soul, but instead present the King with a complete silence from them. On the other hand, if you turn your face, I mean your intellect, in another direction, address and converse with another and clearly turn your back on the unapproachable God, on Whom all the heavenly hosts gaze unblinkingly with fear and trembling, will not He Himself rightly abandon you immediately as someone unworthy who despises Him? But, you say, He is a lover of mankind? I say the same to you as well, but He is so to those who perceive His love for men, and who honor and thank Him worthily. But if, having deemed His love and sweetness as nothing, you incline towards the love of anything else, and wholly bind the impulsion of your soul up in it and take delight in such pleasure, whether food or drink or clothing or a pretty face or gold or silver, or if your soul impresses within you a lust for any other form, then will He Who is pure and holy and without spot, Who has also made you such as He by the Spirit, consent to be with you in any way, you who are so inclined, and will He not immediately abandon you? Of course He will, in every way!

The temptation of the pastorate and its dangers

But if you do none of these, and chase every passion away from you, and throw every evil far away, banish every lust from yourself, abandon every attachment and natural love for friend and kin, and attain to perfect sinlessness and purity, as we have described it above, and—to make myself clear to everyone—possess in addition to these virtues Him entire Who is above the heavens, then neither are you troubled from any direction or leaning away to something else, but you are living with God and your intellect is kept in the Kingdom which is above the heavens. Now, suddenly, someone calls you and shows you a great city with many inhabitants, with houses and palaces varied and vast, with enormous and resplendent temples, priests, high-priests, and an emperor together with the sacred senate and his officers and champions. Then, to speak of no other passion, if by all of these people, I mean the emperor and the officers and the whole multitude of the city, you were invited and besought with tears to accept the care of them, to pastor and edify them, before you had been exhorted to do so by God Who had arranged that you reign together with

Him, and despising Him you abandon what is above and the eternal good things which He had given you in order to live here among what is corruptible and visible with those who have invited you, will He not justly deprive you of all the former and permit you to have your lot and your possessions only in the latter, both while you live and after your departure from the body?

Even if it is He Who calls and orders you to descend to the pastoring of souls, you must fall down before Him and weep, and say to Him with great affliction and fear: "Master, how shall I abandon You and go away to that vain and laborious calling? In no way, Lord! Be not angry with me, Your servant, and do not cast me from such a height into that chaos. No, Master, do not deprive me of this light of Your glory and lead me, worthless and wretched, down to such darkness. Perhaps I have sinned somehow from ignorance, Master, and for that reason, O Compassionate One, You turn me away from where You had so benevolently drawn me up? Do You turn away from me so much, You Who have taken away my many sins and iniquities? But if something has happened and I have sinned, then punish me here. If You command, then cut me up limb from limb, only do not send me out there!"

Accept high office only with God's assurance—and even then with fear

If He then says to you: "Go, pastor My sheep. Go, convert your brothers," you must say to Him once again: "Woe is me, Master, am I the unworthy to be separated from You?" And if He says to you still again: "No, but I shall always be with you", then you must prostrate yourself, must weep and wash His immaculate feet with the tears of your intellect, and say as follows: "How shall You be with me, Master, if I go down there and am darkened? How will You live with me if my heart, which is changeable, is turned by men's flatteries and praises?

How would You accept me if I should be wretchedly exhalted toward pride? How would You not flee, unless I were boldly to reprove kings and mighty ones, injustices and transgressions, for righteousness' sake? How shall I do these and other things so as to please You, and so that You are with me and enabling me, and will not abandon me when I fail and separate Yourself from me, and leave me lying there alone? I am afraid that stinginess, that avarice may take hold of me. I fear that the revolt of the flesh may dominate me, that pleasure may deceive me, that anxiety may darken me, that the honor of rulers and kings may exalt me in a way that is not good, that the burden of rule may puff me up against the brethren, that I may be swept away from what is natural by luxury and drunkenness, that the subtle tissues of my soul may be fattened by over-indulgence, that men's threats may frighten me and render me a transgressor of Your commandments, that the entreaties of brother bishops and friends may make me an accomplice in injustice, or silent about those who work injustice, or that I may become a co-worker of those who do evil and not reprove such people with boldness and demonstrate exertion for the sake of Your commandments. But how might I say it all, Master? Behold, they are indeed innumerable, which You know better than I, Lord. Loving God, do not surrender me to such evils. Because You know what is displeasing about men, their scoffings, reproaches, their slanders, especially of those more knowledgeable and puffed-up by that wisdom of the world which Your grace has abolished. Therefore have mercy on me, Friend of humanity, and do not send me away down there to be tossed about in the midst of evils so great and so many."

These are the things, and yet more than these, which you are obliged to view with suspicion while pleading not to have to descend from heaven to the earth here below. But if the good King and Lover of mankind in His turn, after you have shown your love and humility, says to you again: "Do not fear. Since I have promised to be with you, you will be overcome by none of these adversaries because you will have Me as your helper in every way, and I shall glorify you down there the more greatly, and you shall come back here with a greater and more resplendent radiance, and shall reign with Me for ages without end;" not even then should you be emboldened or completely without anxiety, but with fear and trembling, as one who has been brought down from some great height to a deep cistern full of all kinds of reptiles and wild beasts, ought you to arrive at your metropolitanate, patriarchate, or whatever other rule, whether it be a diocese or the protectorate of a people.

If you do admit that you are not such a person as our discourse has just outlined, but imagine instead that you are ascending to the heights [i.e., of rule] from below, then O, what nerve! O, what darkness! O, what ultimate ignorance! Because these thoughts and attitudes are not those of rational men, but of fools and pagans, or better, of dead men who do not see, do not perceive, do not live, who do not know God at all, nor what awaits us at His future judgement. That, on the one hand, presiding over a flock and taking care for the salvation of our neighbor is an edifying thing, a perfection of the law of love which is the summary of the prophets, no one will deny. And, indeed, Christ thrice repeated the question to Peter whether he loved Him, and after the latter had replied: "Yes Lord, You know that I love You," said: "If you love Me, tend My sheep" [Jn 21:15-17]. On the other hand, that it is not without reflection that one ought to embark upon this ministry, and that it is not just for anyone to attempt, but rather that one is to accomplish it with an exact circumspection and with fear, is completely obvious only to those whose spiritual eye has not been completely darkened. For many, neither knowing what this saying itself means, nor understanding in what way the Lord ordered Peter to tend His sheep, set out—Alas!—audaciously to rule and are not embarrassed at shamelessly presiding over Christ's flock.

On the commandment, "Tend my sheep." Not a social gospel

If you like, however, let us look and consider what this saying is and what it signifies. Is the Lord, on saying to Peter: "Tend My sheep," talking about tending to the needs of earthly life, or indeed, about caring for the things or affairs of life which concern His rational sheep, such that by Peter's care they may be kept healthy, or even that Peter should be provided with a benefice as a voluntary contribution? Or is He saying that the shepherd is to busy himself with their nourishment and provide them with clothing? Is He ordering the Apostle to lead strangers under His roof, or to minister to the infirm, or, once all the faithful have been assembled in the same place, to be concerned with what is required for their feeding and clothing? Most certainly not, not in any way! Because God commanded him to do none of these things. Where is this made clear? From the Lord's very words, for He says to His Apostles: "Take no gold, nor silver...no bag, nor two tunics" [Mt 10:10]. He Who thus lays down a law for them to acquire nothing at all, how could He ever order them to distribute what they do not have to others, or care about such things at all? And again He says: "Take heed to yourselves lest your hearts be weighed down with dissipation and drunkenness and the cares of this life" [Lk 21:34]; and again: "Do not labor for the food which perishes, but for the food which endures to eternal life" [Jn 6:27]. He did not lay it down as law and ordain it just for them, but through them for us as well, and other precepts in addition to these. For He also said:

> Do not be anxious about your life, what you shall eat or what you shall drink, nor about your body, what you

shall put on...Consider the lillies of the field, how they
grow; they neither toil nor spin... [Mt 6:25,28];

and a little later, He says:

Therefore, do not be anxious, saying "What shall we
eat" or "What shall we drink"... For the gentiles seek all
these things, and your heavenly Father knows that you
need them all. But seek first His Kingdom and His
righteousness, and all these things shall be yours as
well. Therefore, be not anxious about tomorrow...
[Mt 6:31-34].

After He had thus said these things, and many more besides,
later on He added to them and said: "And what I say to you, I
say to all" [Mk 13:37].

Therefore, He Who does not allow any to worry about
tomorrow, but commands them to seek the Kingdom of God
alone and its righteousness, how could He ever order His
Apostle, in contradiction to His ordinances, to concern himself
with the feeding and clothing of His sheep, or about protecting
and taking revenge for them and what belongs to them? He
would not, certainly, and He makes this clear in what follows,
for He says: "Behold, I send you out as sheep in the midst of
wolves" [Mt 10:16]; and again:

But I say to you, do not resist one who is evil. But if
anyone strikes you on the right cheek, turn to him the
other also; and if anyone would sue you and take your
coat, let him have your cloak as well...and do not refuse
him who would borrow from you... [Mt 5:39-42].

He, then, Who sent out His own disciples as sheep among
wolves, and laid it down as law to them—and through them, to
us—to turn the other cheek to the man who strikes us on the
right, and to give up our cloak as well to the man who would
sue us for our coat, and not to deny him who would borrow
what is ours, how could He order him who would be tending

His sheep anything at all about vengeance for some earthly affair, or be touched somehow by the concerns for this life, or involve the sheep in such cares and undertakings as He, the Shepherd, had been first commanded to avoid? In no way! And this is what the Apostles themselves confirmed in their works after the Lord's ascension into heaven. For not only did they not pay any attention whatever to their own needs and the needs of those whom they were teaching, but they did not accept either to administer the wealth laid at their feet by those who believed in our Lord Jesus Christ, or take action for the future needs of the brethren regarding food and clothing. As Scripture says, they replied instead:

> It is not right that we should give up the word of God to serve tables. We shall appoint capable men for this, but we will devote ourselves to prayer and to the ministry of the word... [Acts 6:2-4].

Therefore, since it has been demonstrated that we have been commanded not to trouble at all about any earthly affair, neither about our own necessary needs, nor for the defense of either ourselves or our brothers who are wronged and badly used by certain people, let us then go on to examine the meaning of the Lord's saying to the chief of the Apostles: "If you love Me," He said, "more than these, tend My sheep." While I know that this has been made clear from the foregoing, and that many who are intelligent have probably already understood the thrust of the saying, I must impose a little more on your charity[1] for the sake of the ignorant.

Pastors to teach the commandments and exemplify the love of Christ

To tend the sheep is assuredly nothing other than the care of those pastored by word and by teaching, and Christ Himself

---

1   The interlocutor, "your charity," is unknown—see our note 1 to *Discourse* IV, page 19 above, note 2.

showed this when He said to Peter: "How often Satan demanded to have you that he might sift you like wheat, but I have prayed for you that your faith might not fail" [Lk 22:31-32]. Next, He added to this by saying to him: "And when you have turned again, strengthen your brethren" [Lk 22:31-32]. What then does "strengthen your brethren" mean? "From your own example," He says to Peter, "be certain of never being turned back to despair if it should ever happen to your flock that they sin. For what is worse," He continues, "than to have denied Me, the Master of all? But when you had sorrowed and wept bitterly, I immediately reckoned you worthy of compassion and, while you were too timid to stand up for Me, I called you with the rest of the disciples on the mountain, and not even with a single word did I reproach you for that fault. So, then, now that you have yourself returned, strengthen your brothers, pastor My sheep. Pastor them, though, not by leading them back and forth from pasture to pasture and keeping them well-fed and plump in body, nor by enclosing them with fences and walls, but by teaching them to keep everything that I have commanded you, not by honoring some commandments while dismissing others, but by guarding everything that I have commanded you." Then He says:

> Go therefore and make disciples of all nations, baptizing them in the name of the Father and of the Son and of the Holy Spirit, teaching them to observe all that I have commanded you... [Mt 28:19-20];

and He adds: "He who believes and is baptized will be saved; but he who does not believe will be condemned" [Mk 16:16].

"Pastor My sheep." The shepherd of dumb animals does not care about farming, or business, or a house, or abundant tables, or glory, or honor. He is anxious about no other concern of life, neither does he accept being held back by such things at all, but by abandoning house and wife and children he demonstrates his entire concern for his flock. He keeps vigil over it, is sent long distances, has no bed, carries no blanket, but endures outside the burning of the day and suffers the night chill throughout. He is ever in conflict with gales and frost and open air, and he never quits the security and care of his sheep. "But," Christ says, "is it possible for you while at home and on the road, while on your bed and pallet and even while reclining at table, to pastor My sheep? How? By teaching them to have untroubled, sincere, and unhesitating faith in Me, to love Me with all their soul and all their mind, just as I have loved them, too. For I laid down My life and died for their sake. Instead of unreasoning pasturage, set before them the life-giving nourishment of My commandments. Teach them the communion that comes by their doing and fulfilling the commandments. Admonish and exhort them thus hourly to eat their fill, so that they may always be satiated by them and filled with My good things. Provide them with an example of what My good things are and by what deeds they are acquired. Sell your belongings and give alms. Make for yourself a purse which does not grow old, a treasure in heaven which cannot be stolen. Love your enemies. Pray for those who assail you. Do good to those who hate you. Let none of you return evil for evil to anyone. Forgive and you will be forgiven. For, 'If you do not forgive men their trespasses, neither will your heavenly Father forgive you your trespasses' [Mt 6:15]. Be poor in things, so that you may be wealthy in spirit. Despise the glory of this life, so that you may enjoy the one which is in heaven."

The choice is simple: God or the devil

Thus two things are set before us, I mean life and death, and two worlds, the one which is visible and dissolving and the one which is eternal and invisible and indissoluble, the present and the future worlds; and two are they who are active and directly in opposition to each other, I mean God and the devil who opposes Him. And, while the One strives to save us and calls us to life and an eternal kingdom, the other lusts and roars after our destruction and death, and seeks daily for whom he may swallow up through the enjoyment of these temporary things and so make us answerable for everlasting punishment. We must flee the wicked and hostile enemy and escape to the Master Who saves, and invoke His aid, so that we may not be dominated by the prince of darkness and fall to his snares by serving him and sin. And, that the devil is prince of this world and of darkness, listen to Christ Who says: "Behold, the ruler of this world is coming, and in Me he will find nothing" [Jn 14:30]. He is not, however, called "prince" because he has any authority over or is master of the world—away with such blasphemy! he has not even authority over pigs![2]—but because he enslaves those who have nailed themselves to the world through their lust for the wealth and goods which are in it and thus has them under his power. He is called prince of darkness because, having himself fallen from the light at the beginning by his revolt, he will be the eternal heir of darkness. Our God and Master, however, as the Creator and Fashioner of all things, rules with authority by nature over everything in heaven, on earth, and beneath the earth. He is the light unapproachable and without evening, Lord of all things present and to come. Therefore those who obey Him and keep His commandments unbroken, and who enjoy what is temporary in due measure, and who partake of them thankfully and with restraint, are already being led up from them toward what is

2   Cf. Mk 5:11-13 (and parallels in Mt and Lk): the devils expelled by Christ from a demoniac and given leave to possess a herd of swine are unable to keep the animals from plunging over a cliff and perishing. Symeon's imagery here recalls Dt. 30:15ff and, following that lead, a note common to such ancient Christian writings as the *Didache*, *Epistle of Barnabas*, and *Shepherd of Hermas*: "the two ways."

incorruptible and eternal, in that they have been subordinated to the King and God of all and have kept His commandments. As many, however, as practice what is opposed to His commandments, are found as ranked with the adversary and have become God's enemies outright, just as the Savior Himself says: "He who is not with Me is against Me; and he who does not gather with Me scatters" [Lk 11:23].

Litigation is the devil's business, not the Christian pastor's

Beloved, let no one therefore associate with the prince of darkness and ruler of this world. Let no one be ranked with him. Let no one make war with him and his angels against our Savior and God. Let no one go against his own soul, lest he struggle to inherit everlasting fire. Let it not be, I beg you, fathers and brothers and children, let it not be! It is a fearful thing for us to become enemies of God, or even to be thought such. How is it possible for anyone to make war against Christ and do battle for his own damnation? I will tell you here. If someone, whether justly or unjustly, should insult you, or revile you, or slander you, and you do not bear the slight meekly, or, grieved and wounded at heart, you fail to endure it and rein in the movements of your soul, but instead insult in turn the one who insulted you, or revile him, or do something else against him, or, again, do none of these things to him, but instead go away carrying a grudge against him in your heart and do not forgive him with all your soul and pray for him with all your heart, behold! you have at once taken up arms against Christ by doing what is opposed to His ordinances and have become His enemy. You have as well destroyed your own soul by falling in with and putting the seal on your former sins and making them ineradicable. If, again, someone should slap you on your right cheek and you do not turn to him the other, but instead strike him in return, you have become at once a soldier and subordinate of Satan the adversary, and you have struck not just your brother, but, in him, also the One Who said not to strike but to turn the other cheek. And if someone should take gold away from you or something else, whether openly or secretly, whether borrowed or taken by force, and then does not want to give it back to you, whether as an evil-doer or because he does not have the means, and you do not suffer it with thanksgiving and without grudge-bearing, but drag him who has taken it before law courts and hired prosecutors, and ask men for help and present yourself before the tribunal, and are vexed and grieved, leading and dragging your brother along with you, using oaths and perjuries and getting ready to swear and perjure yourself against him, and lying—which is worse than all the rest—and, in addition to all this, hand him over to prison, and both do and practice everything in order to get back what is owed you, how are you not obviously your own worst enemy?

You who have been commanded to visit those in prison and minister to them according to your ability, to make no request of him who has taken what is yours, and give your cloak as well to him who would sue you for your coat, nor this alone, but to lay down your very life unto death for the sake of God's commandment, when you go to court for the sake of lost money and transgress God's precept, when you are grieved, vexed, and consign your brother to prison: are you not obviously insane by angering God and warring against Him, and depriving yourself of eternal life? He who would pastor Christ's flock, therefore, and feed His sheep with the teaching we have described in order to make them fat and fruitful with righteousness, how can he worry about fields at the same time and engage in concern for possessions, go to court for them and frighten off those who would abuse them unjustly, sometimes approaching the judge and sometimes resisting controversies and lies, and sometimes even becoming himself responsible for oaths and perjuries? For it is necessarily the case, given that the pastor is telling the truth, that his opponents in court will lie and take oaths and commit open perjury. But, if this is the way things happen, how will such things be bearable to the soul that loves God, or how will the people involved be pleasing to the God Who said: "But I say to you, do not swear at all...but let what you say be simply 'Yes' or 'No'; anything more than this comes from the evil one" [Mt 5:34, 37]; and again: "Amen, amen I tell you, on the day of judgement men will render account for every idle word" [Mt 12:26].

Final warnings and exhortation

If I have persuaded you to obey the truth of Christ and His words, let it not then be the case that you run off to positions of rulership and government over others for the sake of human glory and luxury and bodily enjoyment. Fear the judgement of God and that dreadful verdict which God pronounced through the prophet Ezekiel[3] against those who were pastoring His sheep unworthily:

> Thus says the Lord Adonai: Ho, shepherds of Israel who have been feeding yourselves! Should not shepherds feed the sheep? You eat the milk, you clothe yourselves with the wool, you slaughter the fatlings; but you do not feed the sheep. The weak you have not strengthened, the sick you have not healed, the crippled you have not bound up, those who fare poorly you have not made firm, the strayed you have not brought back, the lost you have not sought, and the strong you have ruled with force and harshness and derision. And My sheep were scattered because there were no shepherds [Ezek 34:2-5];

and a little later:

> Thus says the Lord Adonai: Behold, I am against the shepherds; and I will require My sheep at their hand, and put a stop to their feeding My sheep [Ezek 34:10];

and again:

> But if the watchman sees the sword coming, and does

---

3 Symeon in fact mistakenly refers to Joel. We have taken the liberty of correcting him.

not blow the trumpet, and the sword comes and takes away the life of any one of them; that man is taken away for the sake of his own sin, but his blood I will require at the watchman's hand [Ezek 33:6].

O brothers, these are fearful and most dreadful things!

On account of this let us first of all strive rather to pastor ourselves well as Christ's flock, as a royal priesthood, and subject our flesh to the Spirit, so that that which is better in us may prevail over what is worse. And whensoever we should enter into the depths of humility and wash away from ourselves the stains of sin with the waves of our tears, we shall acquire an attitude of mourning, a spirit which is meek and calm, and, by our great thirst for God's righteousness, we shall be filled full of the inexpressible good things of His Kingdom through the advocacy of the Holy Spirit. Next, having recovered thus the bowels of mercy and compassion, we shall acquire a pure heart in perfect dispassion and shall see the light of God, which is to say the Spirit Himself, working and declaring within us the hidden mysteries of God's Kingdom. Once we have joined what is apart in ourselves into one by virtue of profound peace, we shall also be at peace with ourselves, and perfect, as a single harmonious instrument in body and soul and in the one Spirit. Nor is this all, but when, after many tribulations and calamities, many trials, we wait patiently upon Christ and endure while being persecuted, and entreat while we are blasphemed, and bless while being cursed, not reckoning up evil to anyone in any way but covering all, enduring all, by the foundations of the virtues keeping our steadiness unshaken, and thus by means of and through all that we have said, when we have grown into the maturity which is according to Christ and have arrived at perfect manhood, at the measure of the stature of Christ's fulness, in perfect knowledge of God and in the wisdom of the words and mysteries which are provided by the all-Holy Spirit, then indeed let us devote ourselves to the benefit of others, as the least of servants, even though we are in fact called from above in accord with the Lord's own voice: "Whoever would be first among you, he must be last of all and servant of all" [Mk 9:35].

But, so long as we have not attained to this degree by our many struggles, let us devote our time—I beseech you all—to being subordinate to our fathers in God, and to God Himself Who holds all together, daily repenting and being cleansed by the tears which are for God's sake, so that we may be enabled to know Him and to know that He does not lie but gives what He has promised to those who love Him and keep His divine commandments. It is He Who, indeed, will give to each his reward according to his works when He hands the Kingdom and the subjection of all things to the Father, to Whom is due all glory, honor, and worship, now and ever, and unto ages of ages. Amen.

TWELFTH ETHICAL DISCOURSE

Introduction

Discourse XII begins the concluding four discourses which are quite different in tone from the preceding. There is no note of controversy. In this short treatise Symeon offers his interpretation of a phrase from Ephesians 5:16, "redeeming the time of our present lives." He illustrates the scriptural verse with an extended image of merchants in the world either "redeeming" the time of their lives with profitable activity or else wasting it in idleness. The Christian is to redeem his or her time on earth by reckoning death no great price for eternal life, and so by pursuing patiently the struggle against temptation, the "mind of the flesh," and for the acquisition of the virtues.

ON THE SAYING OF THE APOSTLE: "REDEEMING THE TIME, BECAUSE THE DAYS ARE EVIL" [EPH 5:16]

Nothing whatever is more profitable for the soul which has chosen to study God's law day and night than searching the divine scriptures. The meaning of the Holy Spirit's grace is hidden in them. It fills a man's spiritual perception with every pleasure, lifts it entirely from earthly things and the lowliness of what is visible, and makes it both angelic in form and a sharer in the angels' very life. But let us take a look at what the divine Apostle talks about with us every day, and let us examine some of his God-inspired words carefully, so that we may be enriched with the wealth that is stored up in them and nourished by them with the grace of the Spirit unto the unfailing gladness and enjoyment of our souls. What is it, then, which we are to interpret? That which Paul urges on us when he says: "Redeeming the time, because the days are evil." Now, when we have examined what happens in daily life, we should also be able to learn what this text signifies. For just as every merchant and craftsman and farmer, and indeed everyone who approaches any craft whatever, requires the greatest care and attention for his work, to the degree that if he fails to pay attention to it for even a little while, one brief hour, he sustains a great loss, so does the same apply to spiritual struggles, works, and practices.

The example of merchants at a fair

But let us provide your charity with a more detailed example from one of these men of business.[1] If the merchants are all running off to the festival to do some business and profit from their commerce, but one of them sees some in front of him and others behind him hurrying to catch up, or if, sitting in front of his house, he sees them passing by and going off in a hurry to the festival but is himself held back by indolence or laziness, or worse, is also preoccupied with drunkeness and luxury and is moreover wretchedly enthralled by the charms of a prostitute, and consequently chooses not to run to business, he wastes day after day. Have not the first redeemed the time of their lives by doing business and returning with great profit, and has the other man not lost that time by spending it on things which are vain and profitless, thus in effect selling it for nothing? Or, if he should arrive at the fair with the others and, while they, having money, immediately go off to business, each one of them buying something from which he hopes to make a profit for himself, he on the other hand, who has no money at all, runs around looking for a way to borrow some so that he, too, can

---

1   Again, "your charity" is unknown. See note 2 to *Discourse* IV, page 19 above.

do business, and if the fair should conclude before he has found any to borrow and he is left without having done any trading, has not he as well wasted his time by going to the fair without money? Or, if he does arrive at the fair with money, yet drops his urge to do business and begins to circulate instead among the booths of the liquor salesmen, or of the cooks, or sellers of other foods, and eats and drinks greedily now at the one, now at the others, and indeed wastes all his money on drunkenness and debauch, has he not, too, lost his time and stupidly squandered all his wealth?

There is also the man who arrives at the fair and does none of these harmful things. But, if after entering in the company of his fellow merchants, he is content to go around inspecting and learning who is there whom he knows and whom he does not know, who is familiar and who a stranger, and how each of them does business while he himself does none whatever, and thus the fair concludes and everyone goes home while he is still wandering about, have not those who did business eagerly redeemed their time by doing with it what is appropriate and so getting a profit for themselves, while he who was so curious about others' affairs and failed to do any business, even though he accompanied the others, has he not wasted his time by not having taken any profit from going to the fair? Again, if some, for the sake of gain, should hold in contempt the danger of thieves on the road and the journey's effort and the distance of travel, while another, taken by the fear of these things, should refuse to accompany the others even though he is begged by them to do so and hears their promises of protection from the dangers he foresees, have not the former redeemed their time by doing good business and making a profit while the latter has foolishly wasted it because he was afraid of danger where there was none?

Everlasting life is the real bargain

It is certainly the same with respect to every spiritual practice and activity. Whenever others walk in God's commandments and diligently and zealously work on the virtues while we carry on in idleness and inattention, it is the former who have redeemed their time and been benefited the greatest, and it is we who have lost both our time and ourselves. But, let us take another look at this idea. What does he mean by saying: "Redeeming the time, because the days are evil"? How does someone redeem his time, and who is he, and what are the evil days on account of which we ought to redeem the time? The time of every man's activity is the time of this present life, and the days of this life are obviously evil for those who do not use them well. Thus everyone who conducts himself soberly and justly with a healthy attitude in this life, and who bears with courage and patience the pains and sorrows of those trials and tribulations which come upon him, whether from visible or invisible enemies, wisely redeems his time and makes good use of the evil days of the present life. To make this yet more clear, I will direct my remarks to what occurs in daily life.

Whenever tribulations and curses and dishonors and gibes come down on the man who knows how to deal well with the present time, he seizes them as one who knows these things and is aware of the benefits to be derived from them, and he takes them on his shoulders and goes his way rejoicing. He puts down patience alone instead of gold as payment, and thus in a single instant he redeems the time which others are unable to find, or seize, or gain through many years of fasting, keeping vigil, sleeping on the ground, and working hard at home. The man who does not, however, know how to do business in this way loses the time of his salvation. But, if you like, let us continue with still another illustration. Two people are forcefully encouraged by someone to transgress God's commandment. If one of them, out of timidity and fear of the punishments and torments which will come upon him in future, takes refuge in flight and runs away and hides himself, while the other is brave and suffers many tortures for the sake of God's commandment, or even undergoes death itself, which of these two has redeemed the time? The one who hid and fled from tribulations, or the one who suffered and endured much, and perhaps even died? It is clearly obvious that the man who endured the tribulations and did not refuse death is the one who has redeemed the time, while the other lost both the time and his soul's salvation.

It is assuredly thus that those who think correctly purchase the eternal good things and everlasting joy, through the trials and tribulations which are in this life, and through the death of the body they win that eternal and immortal life and habitation which is with the immortal and everlasting God. And, just as the merchant who finds many precious things being sold for a small price, say for a single obol or nomisma, hurries to pay it with joy so he can take possession of those precious things, so, too, does the man who is struggling for the sake of God's commandments joyfully hurry to choose death, so that by means of a single obol—I mean death—he may acquire the everlasting good things that are to come. Those who love the world are not like this. Not so are the lovers of life, of glory, of the flesh, of pleasure and of wealth. When they are invited to transgress God's commandment by someone who happens to be prominent in the world, unable to endure that person's irritation or loss of respect or rejection and the loss of wealth entailed, they betray what is eternal and priceless and foolishly purchase what is temporary and corruptible and worthless, and so lose their own salvation, eternal life itself. Those, too, who prefer to purchase for themselves a few days of comfort trade the time of the present life in exchange for infinite punishment.

In order that we not suffer the same fate, let us, I beg you, redeem the present life so long as the fair of our life continues, because its days are exceedingly evil. Ten thousand are the waves of bitter sin which daily surge against us, sometimes filling our soul with dizziness and vertigo by means of the body's excitability and its disordered impulses, and sometimes, through the enemies visible and invisible who set themselves against us, instilling in us and agitating our hearts toward despair and lust and wild anger, and by means of these taking us altogether far from the Kingdom of God.

The purchase of the virtues

Therefore, let us redeem the time of our life, giving over our resolution and our whole selves to the doing of God's commandments alone, to the sole acquisition and gain of the virtues, so that, carried by the gifts of the Spirit, we may arrive at God's safe harbors, and may flee those evil days and that evil report which sends sinners away to the outer fire prepared for the devil and his angels.

Let us redeem our soul's thinking by despising what is visible and by the study and doing of what is better; and let us flee the mind of the flesh, which cannot please God, nor indeed can snatch us from the enjoyment of what is temporary and guide our thought toward what abides and is eternal, which does not allow the one so ruled by it to seek the things of God, but drags the soul down instead toward the bestial impulses of the flesh and makes man bestial altogether.

Let us redeem our righteousness, by which we become accustomed to being with God, distinguishing with all piety and discernment what is unjust from what is just, and preferring virtue to evil, and allowing no entry or freedom of approach to the evil one toward our own destruction and damnation, but allotting what is due in justice to each, to the body, on the one hand, providing the necessary nourishment and shelter, and to the soul, on the other, giving all our might for its nourishment with divine meditation, with prayers, with tears, and for its purification as a receptacle of the divine light of God Who is Himself the sun of righteousness, Who will also justify us by the gift of His Holy Spirit and show us forth as righteous in union with Him, and make us communicants of the unspeakable good things of His Kingdom.

Let us redeem the courage of our own souls through much patient endurance of trials, in accordance with the Lord's own words: "By your endurance," He says, "you will possess your souls" [Lk 21:9]. Clearly, this means that by taking our stand with a courageous attitude against sin, and by striking at the enemy with the weapons of the Spirit, we suffer our ills as good soldiers of Christ: in fasting, in vigils, in sleeping on the ground, in prayers, in mourning, in sackcloth and repentance and continued petitions, in order that we may take up the crowns of victory and reign together with Christ.

Let us redeem the sobriety of our body with all continence and humility, because he who contests according to the rules and competes in the stadium of piety is in every way continent, according to the Apostle [I Cor 9:25]. For if we acquire this sobriety, we shall flee the evil days of irrational lust, and anger, and from the flesh itself as true enemy of the Spirit [cf. Gal 5:16-24]. We shall flee the defilement which attaches to the soul, the condemnation of the conscience, the impurity of heart, the unfavorable opinion of men, the turning away of God Himself, and we shall gain great things by means of this spiritual "transaction," doing prudent business with the time of the present life, traversing the path of this life in righteousness and sobriety, bearing bravely, that is, the burden and the heat of the day.

In so doing business with the present time, giving way in what is temporary to those who desire it and contending instead for what is alone incorruptible and eternal, we shall arrive, richly provided for by the Spirit, at the calm haven of God's Kingdom. And we shall not fear either that evil report which drives the sinners into the outer fire, nor those evil torments and the dreadful day and condemnation of the judgement, in that we bring as our dowry the most precious pearl of the Spirit, which we have found and purchased by dedicating our will, our purposes, our intentions, and our powers to the business of the time of the present life. To which same may we all attain, wisely dealing with the time of our present life, by the grace and love for mankind of our Lord Jesus Christ, to Whom be glory with the Father and the Holy Spirit, now and ever, and unto ages of ages. Amen.

THIRTEENTH ETHICAL DISCOURSE

Introduction

Discourse XIII takes up the Pauline contrast in I Corinthians 15:47 between the man of dust, Adam, and the heavenly man, Christ. Symeon recalls the Fall of the first man, created to enjoy the company of angels and to look on God, and his loss of the "robe of divine glory" and reduction to the sensate life of the other animals. The children of Adam grew still more sinful and, when they had reached the nadir of idolatry and slavery to the devil, the Word of God took flesh from "the side" of Adam, that is, from Eve through the Theotokos (the discussion recalls *Discourse* II, in Vol. I), and built it into the perfect man. He is now the true mediator between God and men, granting us through faith and the Holy Spirit a share in Himself. To share in the life of the Heavenly Man we are called to be faithful to Him, become like Him in virtue. This cannot be accomplished without repentance, the recognition of sins, and the confession which a merciful God has provided for us. Thus we may be reconciled to Him and recover the boldness (*parresia*) which Adam had with his Creator, and speak to him as "friend to friend," and see Him clearly. This is no dream but rather, Symeon concludes, "is exceedingly possible (*lian dynaton*)."

ON THE SAYING OF THE APOSTLE: "THE FIRST MAN WAS FROM EARTH, OF DUST; THE SECOND MAN, THE LORD, IS FROM HEAVEN" [I COR 15:47]

The blessed Paul has feasted us well at the earlier meal of his

words and has made our hearts glad. Now he has set out for us
another course of feasting on his God-inspired sayings, full on
the one hand of spiritual food which our inner man knows to
be for his nourishment, at once gladdened and strengthened at
heart with the living bread of the Word and with the wine which
rejoices us with the wisdom and knowledge of God, full on the
other hand as well with the divine grace of the Spirit through
which the soul is filled with every joy and delight, and leaves
behind the lower things of life and ascends toward heaven and
God with the nimble wings of thought. Let us therefore see what
this table of the Apostle is, and what its food. But, let us first
lift up our minds from what is earthly and perishable. Let us
pay attention with all care to what is said as people about to
listen to God's own words, so that we may be rightly accounted
worthy of feasting together with the Spirit Who, through the
Apostle, declares the hidden mysteries of the heavenly Kingdom. He says: "The first man was from earth, of dust; and the
second man, the Lord, is from heaven" [I Cor 15:47]. My
beloved, do not simply skip past this word and assume it to be
self-evident, for a great depth of thought lies within it which
requires much interpretation and attention. Rather, keep your
hearing at the ready, and enter into the depths of God's mysteries hidden within it:

The man of dust: Adam and the loss of glory

> The first man was from earth, of dust; the second man,
> the Lord, from heaven. As was the man dust, so are
> those who are of the dust; and as is the man of heaven,
> so are those who are of heaven [I Cor 15:47-48].

He says that Adam was the first man and of dust, as it is
written: "The Lord God formed man taking dust from the
ground" [Gen 2:7]. So, being made of dust from the earth, and
having received a breath of life which the word calls an intelligent soul and the image of God, he was placed in the garden

to work and given a commandment to keep. How so? So that, as long as he did keep it and work, he would remain immortal and compete everlastingly with the angels, and together with them would praise God unceasingly and receive His illuminations and see God intelligibly, and hear His divine voice. But, in that same hour that he should transgress the commandment given him and eat of the tree from which God had commanded him not to eat, he would be given over to death and be deprived of the eyes of his soul. He would be stripped of his robe of divine glory; his ears would be stopped up, and he would fall from his way of life with the angels and be chased out of paradise. This indeed did happen to the transgressor, and he fell from his eternal and immortal life. For once Adam had transgressed God's commandment and lent his ear for the deceitful devil to whisper in, and was persuaded by him on hearing his cunning words against the Master Who had made him, he tasted of the tree and, perceiving with his senses, he both saw and beheld with passion the nakedness of his body. He was justly deprived of all those good things. He became deaf. With ears become profane he could no longer listen to divine words in a manner which was spiritual and adequate to God, as such words resound only in those who are worthy. Neither could he see the divine glory any longer, in that he had voluntarily turned his intellect away from it and had looked upon the fruit of the tree with passion, and had believed the serpent who said: "In that now that you eat of it, you will be as gods, knowing good and evil" [Gen 3:5].

Thus was the man of dust deceived by a hope for deification. Partaking of the fruit, he was entirely deprived of all those good and heavenly things and was lowered to the impassioned sensations of earthly and visible creatures. And, to repeat myself, he became deaf, blind, insensible in relation to that from which he had fallen. At once become mortal, corruptible and irrational, he became like the beasts which are without intelligence, in accordance with the prophet who cried: "He is become like the beasts without intellect and is like them" [Ps 49:12, cf. LXX 48:13]. Have you learned from what sort of glory, and what kind of way of life, and what sort of food, and to what dishonor man was brought down; to what shame and ignorance, to what poverty he had fallen who was abundantly wealthy? Such did he become and so he was, though we have not been able to say everything about the first man, who is from earth, of dust.

The man of heaven: Christ the incarnate Word

Now let us see and be taught also by the divine Scripture of what sort the second man is, the Lord, from heaven. The latter is God from God, the Begotten without beginning of a Father without beginning: bodiless of bodiless, incomprehensible of incomprehensible, eternal of eternal, inaccessible of inaccessible, unapproachable of unapproachable, immortal of immortal, invisible of invisible, Word of God and God, by Whom all things were made both in heaven and on earth and, that I may put it briefly, so being and abiding in the Father, and possessing the Father abiding in Himself, Who, neither as separate from the Father nor as wholly abandoning Him, came down to earth and was incarnate of the Holy Spirit and Mary the Virgin and became man, without change becoming our equal in all things save sin, so that, traversing all that which is ours, He might re-forge and make that first man anew and, through him, all of us who were begotten and came into being from him and are like him who engendered us. Since, because Adam who engendered us had become corruptible and mortal—and, I will add, deaf and blind—and, by reason of his transgression, both naked and insensible of his divine vesture, such being the man of dust, so as well have they all become who were born of him: of dust, corruptible, mortal, deaf, blind, naked and insensible, differing in no way from the irrational animals or, better, become even worse than the beasts as having embraced all the latters' passions and taken them into themselves.

To such ignorance of God and His divine commandments were they brought down who were begotten of dust from the man of dust, that the honor which they ought to have rendered to God they gave instead to this visible creation, and not just to earth and sky and sun, moon and stars, fire and water and the rest, but they even made gods of those shameful passions themselves which ought not even to be imagined, let alone practiced, and which God had forbidden them. These they set up and—O, the shamelessness!—worshipped as gods. What were they? Fornication, adultery, homosexuality, murder, and whatever else is similar which, not God—away with the blasphemy!—but the devil enjoins and suggests and approves, by which the whole race of mankind was and is enslaved, by which the devil has made and makes us his slaves and subject to his control. Whence, even if there were someone among those thousands and tens of thousands who had not stooped to these shameful ordinances and precepts, since he, too, because of his descent from the seed of those who had sinned, was yet a slave of the tyrant, death, he would also be given over to its corruption and sent without mercy to hell.[1] There was no one, you see, who was able to save and redeem him. For this very reason, therefore, God the Word Who had made us had pity on us and came down. He became man, not by intercourse and the emission of seed—for the latter are consequences of the Fall—but of the Holy Spirit and Mary the Ever-Virgin. Having assumed flesh

1   Here again, as in *Discourse* VI (see page 76, note 9 above), we find a typically Greek patristic understanding of "original sin." It is the rule of the tyrant and usurper, death (as in Rom 5:12), or of "him who has the empire [*kratos*] of death, that is the devil" (Heb 2:14). See J. Meyendorff, *Byzantine Theology*, 143-149.

endowed with a soul from her all-immaculate blood, He became man and was Himself called and became flesh, He Who is Son and Word of God, without change or alteration, as it is written: "And the Word became flesh and tabernacled among us" [Jn 1:14]. This is the miracle which is incomprehensible and inconceivable to all, that He Himself both remained unchangably in His divinity and became perfect man.

For just as God formed Adam from the earth and endowed him with a breath of life, and he became a perfect and living soul without intercourse or emission of seed, so did the One Who had made him become a man without intercourse or emission. And just as it is written there in the Old Testament that God put Adam into a deep trance and, while he slept, took one of his ribs and built it up and made the woman, so He did also in the New Testament. How? In what way? Adam's rib is the woman. Thus, from this rib of Adam, which is to say from the woman herself, God the Word took flesh endowed with a soul and built it up into a perfect man, in order that He might become a son in truth of Adam. Having thus taken the title of man and become like us in all things except for sin, He became immediately akin to all men according to the flesh. This was also said by someone else among our predecessors: "When He clothed Himself with flesh, He also put on brotherhood."[2] But, being Himself at once God and man, His flesh and soul were and are holy—and beyond holy. God is holy, just as He was and is and shall be, and the Virgin is immaculate, without spot or stain, and so, too, was that rib which was taken from Adam. However, the rest of humanity, even though they are His brothers and kin according to the flesh, yet remained even as they were, of dust, and did not immediately become holy and sons of God. Now, pay exact attention to what the Spirit is saying in the following: God became man and took on the title

2   G.Nyssa, *Cont.Eunom.* XII, *PG* 45.885B.

of kin and brother of all men. The Son of God alone is both God and man, was and is alone holy—as He shall be forever—alone is righteous, alone true, alone immortal, alone the lover of mankind, alone merciful and compassionate, alone sovereign, alone light of the world, He Who is the light unapproachable.

Faith and obedience to the commandments mediate participation in the man of heaven

Since this is what He is and we, on the other hand, lie in death and corruption, and have no communion whatever with Him unless, as we have said, it be our kinship according to the flesh, then it is faith in Him which mediates between both—I mean between God and man—so that, although we are poor and possess nothing whatever by which we may enter into our salvation, God has mercy and accepts our faith in Him in place of everything else, and so freely grants us forgiveness of our sins, deliverance from death and corruption, and freedom. The latter, indeed, He bestows to the present time on those who believe in Him with all their soul, nor just that, but as well everything else which He has promised and promises us daily in His holy Gospels. So, what are these things? That He will make us new and born again by water and the Spirit, will number us with His servants, the saints, will provide us with the grace of the Holy Spirit Himself, and will allow us to partake through the Spirit in the good things of the earth which the meek shall inherit in gladness and rejoicing of heart, and will Himself be united and joined with us, and both will become one in Him and in God the Father Who will bind us to the Spirit.

We therefore enter into participation and enjoyment of all those things when we observe exactly everything that He has commanded us and, in turn, when we flee everything we have been forbidden and do not turn back to it, like dogs to their vomit. Then, assuredly, if we keep everything which God has

said and says to us, we are truly faithful, proving our faith by
our deeds, and we become as He is, holy and perfect, altogether
heavenly, children of the heavenly God, by grace and adoption
like Him in all things, since He has Himself borne our name
and become like us except for sin. If, though, by holding His
holy and life-giving commandments in contempt, we draw
away through negligence and do something contrary to His
precepts, do what we have been commanded not to do, then we
fall away immediately from all those good things which were
given us through Baptism. And, just as Adam after the Fall is
cast out of paradise and stripped naked of the food and company of the angels, and departs from the sight of God, so are
we, too, separated from the Church of His holy servants when
we sin, and on account of sin we take off the divine vesture,
Christ Himself, which we had put on in Baptism. Nor this
alone, but we are deprived of eternal life itself and the unfading
light, are deprived of the everlasting good things, of sanctification and adoption to sonship. We become thus once again of
dust, as that first man was of dust, instead of heavenly and like
the second man, the Lord Jesus Christ, in all things. In addition,
we also become subject to death and to darkness once more,
and are sent away to the unquenchable fire to be tortured with
great weeping and gnashing of teeth. For it is not from a
material paradise that we are cast out now, as was Adam,
neither are we condemned to till the earth like he was, but it is
from the Kingdom of heaven and those good things of which
it is written: "What no eye has seen, nor ear heard, nor the heart
of man conceived" [I Cor 2:9], that we cast ourselves out and
so make ourselves liable to gehenna, and, unless recall through
repentance were allowed us, no one would ever be saved.

Repentance and confession are necessary: God does not lie

For this reason, then, God who is the lover of humanity and
merciful, and Who wills our salvation, has wisely placed re-

pentance and confession between Himself and us, and He has given authority to everyone who desires it to recall himself from his fall, and, through these [repentance and confession], to enter again into his earlier familiarity, his glory and boldness before God; and, not just this, but also, if he should wish to give proof of an ardent repentance, to become himself once more an heir of those good things spoken of, or of things which are greater still. For according to the degree of his repentance, every man will find a corresponding boldness and familiarity with God, and will find this happening consciously and visibly, and as one friend to another friend will converse with Him face to face, and will see Him plainly with the eyes of the intellect. Therefore, those who after baptism do not possess such familiarity and boldness with all assurance, nor share in the good things mentioned, nor know that they are clothed with Christ, nor behold the light of His divinity in the light of the Spirit: let them pry into their conscience and, when they have scrupulously examined it, they will find that they have set aside, whether in whole or in part, the covenants which they made for all time at their Baptism. But, if not this, then they will find that they have dug a hole for the talent of sanctification and adoption to sonship which was given them and have not put it to work, and it is for this reason that they are deprived of the sight of God, since He does not lie nor repent of His gifts. For He said: "He who loves Me will keep My commandments, and I shall love him and manifest Myself to him" [Jn 14:21].

You have heard what the Master says: "He who loves Me will keep My commandments, and I shall love him and manifest Myself to him." [Jn 14:21] If then Christ is truth, as He Himself says about Himself: "I am the truth" [Jn 14:6], and the truth cannot lie—for the Apostle says that "It is impossible that God should prove false" [Heb 6:18]—then let no one of those who do not see the Lord say that this is impossible! Because it is not impossible. On the contrary, it is exceedingly possible! For if Christ says: "I am the light of the world" [Jn 8:12], those who do not see Him are outright blind. They are obviously blind and have remained so because they have not loved Him and kept His commandments. If they had loved Him and kept His commandments, then they would have longed to see Him, would have sought after this with all their soul, and He Who is not false, but is by nature true and the truth, would have manifested Himself to them [cf. Jn 14:21]. For this reason He came into the world, in order to illumine everyone in it, everyone, that is, who lies in darkness, and illumine them not with some light alien to Him, but with the light of His own glory and divinity. Therefore, let no one of the faithful who does not see the Lord in his intellect, who is not plainly and consciously illumined by His light, nor abides always in the contemplation of His glory and, in this abiding, sees God within himself, say that this is impossible. Let him not utter this, and talk as if he were an infidel. Instead, beloved, when you have examined your own conscience, as we have said, you will find yourself responsible for your deprivation of the Master and the sight of His glory.

So, you should repent and grieve for yourself. Whenever you do find yourself in this condition, and find that you have deprived yourself of such great and so many good things, and have fallen from the glory and contemplation of the Kingdom of heaven, then make haste by repentance and confession to attain to the good things which are eternal, in Christ Jesus our Lord, to Whom be glory and majesty, together with the Father and the Holy Spirit forever. Amen.

FIFTEENTH ETHICAL DISCOURSE

Introduction

Discourse XV, on monastic withdrawal or *hesychia* (literally "quiet"), provides a fitting conclusion, particularly in view of the movement which would take this name some three centuries after Symeon's death and which would make significant use of his writings. The New Theologian provides several models of true *hesychia*, including the disciples around Christ at the Transfiguration on Mt Tabor, Moses on Mt Sinai—both traditional images of the encounter with God and both as well central to the hesychast movement and theology of the fourteenth century—and the company of the Eleven meeting Christ in the upper room (Jn 20). Unless, he warns, one does encounter the living Christ, then one's seclusion is to no purpose. He goes on to declare that merely "outward withdrawal" is not the key. The true meaning of *hesychia* is an inward one, the fulfillment of the commandments and knowledge of God which derives therefrom. This is also the true and unique foundation of apostolic work. Symeon thus concludes with the warning note which has informed most of the discourses: those who do presume to teach without this experience can look forward to a terrible reckoning on the Day of Judgment.

ON WITHDRAWAL [HESYCHIA]

Since I intend to speak a little about the most perfect of the virtues, I beg you to open your ears to me, you who long for this to some degree and have prepared yourself beforehand to climb up to its summits by your progress and ascent along the way of the other virtues. Pay close attention, that is, to what I say, so that, when you have learned of its work through my words, you may hasten to present yourselves as worthy of its reception and practice by your longing for its merit and wealth. So, I shall begin here and, for the sake of him who is a lover of this virtue, will cut short the opening of my discourse.

Models of Hesychia: Thekla, the sinful woman, Mount Tabor, Moses, the Upper Room

Let him who is keeping silence and remaining alone in his cell be like the proto-martyr Thekla.[1] She sat at her window with ears only for St Paul's teaching. She thus was removed from earthly things and the body's needs, because, as her *Life* says, she did not leave her seat but, glued like a spider to her window, got up neither to eat nor drink, but only listened to Paul. She pursued him when he left her region, took flight and left her parents and fiancé and everything else behind. She sought and ran after him whom alone she desired, permitting herself the memory of no one else except for Paul. So greatly, indeed, had the desire for Paul taken hold of her that, circling the place where he had sat to teach, she kissed the ground where his feet had stood. Let nothing here seem curious to you. Instead, if you have not discovered the why of it, then look for it and you will find it.

---

[1] For the story of Thekla, see *PG* 115.824D. This popular tale of the virgin imitator of St Paul comes from Christian antiquity, perhaps the second or third century. For Symeon's acquaintance with such apocryphal literature, the favorite reading of devout believers from late antiquity throughout the Byzantine period, see B. Krivocheine, "*Ho anhyperephanos theos:* Symeon the New Theologian and early Christian Popular Piety," *SP* 2 (1957): 485-494.

Let him be, if he will, like the prostitute and cling with his intellect to the Lord's feet, kissing them and washing them with his tears, and looking away to no one else except to Him Who is able to forgive him his sins. Let him also be like the maid servant whose eyes are on the hands of her mistress,[2] himself also gazing without blinking at the hands of his Lord and God. Let him be like a bride, lying down in union with Christ the Bridegroom and rising with Him to life everlasting—or, better, abiding always in Him and carrying Him always abiding in himself. Let him be, if he is able, even like one of the officials who is present with the emperor inside the latter's chambers, conversing with the Lord in confidence, and speaking with his Master face to face as a friend.

Let him who is solitary [lit., keeps silence] be like those who ascended Mt Thabor with Jesus [cf. Mt 17:1ff] and who saw His radiance flash with light like lightening, and His raiment changed, and the light of His face; who saw the bright cloud and heard the Father's voice say: "This is My beloved Son," and who, astounded, fell down prostrate on their faces.[3] Let him be able to say, as did Peter: "Lord, it is good for us to be here. Let us build three tabernacles, for You and for Your Father and for Your Holy Spirit, for the one Kingdom, for an

2   This is a citation from Psalm 123:2, sung regularly today as one of the two psalm verses intercalcated among the aposticha (hymn verses in the latter part of the service) in daily vespers. Thus, perhaps, we have another allusion to the regular worship of the monastery.

3   Symeon includes Mt Tabor, site of Christ's transfiguration (cf. Mk 9:2ff and parallels in Mt and Lk) according to the tradition, among the models of the "quiet life," i.e., life in monastic retreat. This is especially significant in view of Tabor's prominance in the controversy over the uncreated light of the transfiguration in the fourteenth century. For Symeon's mysticism of "light," see our *Introduction*, Part II, in vol. III, forthcoming.

eternal dwelling of soul and body and intellect, constructing them through purification and raising them on high with the variety of the virtues." Or, like those sitting in the upper room in Jerusalem, let him, too, receive the power from on high. Or, indeed, having like them received the visitation of the Comforter, let the fleshly minded think him filled with new wine, and let them consider him an idle boaster and as one who is arrogant beyond his station, because he brings forth new things and interprets ancient teachings, and speaks with tongues, and overturns the words of those who contradict the Spirit's teachings [cf. Acts 2:2-13].

Let him also be like Moses on the peak of the mountain, going up alone and himself entering into the cloud, hidden away from others' eyes. If he becomes such a one, he will not just see the "back parts,"[4] but will be consciously present before the face of God and, looking on God Himself alone and being seen by Him in turn, and hearing His voice, he will be instructed in the mystery of the heavenly Kingdom, and then will set down the law for others. He will be enlightened, and will lighten others with the light of knowledge. He will be shown mercy, and will be merciful in return. This man asks and receives, and when he has received, gives in turn to those who ask him. He is loosed from the bond of evils, and himself looses others in turn.

---

4   The reference here is to Exodus 33:18-23, a frequent image for the fathers of the encounter with God (cf. Gregory Nazianzus, *Theo. Or.* II.1; Gregory Nyssa, *Life of Moses* 16; and Dionysius Areopagita, *MT* I.3 above). Symeon, however, parts company with the Gregories and joins—perhaps—with Dionysius in insisting that the vision is not limited just to God's "back parts." For Moses in the cloud with God as an image of the monk in his cell, cf. the *Apophegmata Pateron,* Macarius 36: "...the cell of the monk is the furnace of Babylon where the three youths found the Son of God; and [it is] the pillar of cloud within which God spoke to Moses."

Let him who keeps silence well be like those who sat within with the doors closed for fear of the Jews. And, when he has seen Jesus enter—or, better, knows that He is within him Who is everywhere present—let him ask and receive peace from Him Who gives it. Rather, indeed, let him welcome the Holy Spirit with fear and trembling from Him Who breathes It [cf. Jn 20:19-23]. Let him see precisely and thoroughly feel with the intelligible hands of his intellect and the perceptions of his soul whether He is indeed Himself the God over all. For He will not be irritated by his inquiries, but, accepting his praise-worthy timidity, will say to him such things as these: "Why are you troubled? Why do questionings rise in your heart? [Lk. 24:39] Peace be to you! I AM, do not be afraid. See the glory of My divinity. Handle Me and know that it is I Myself. Taste and see that he who is darkness and takes the form of an angel of light to the imagination—and not in truth—neither has nor certainly can create in you any goodness, nor sweetness, nor joy and freedom, nor tranquility of being, nor intelligible perception and illumination of soul such as you see in Me Who both am these things and Who make them present in you."[5]

True silence derives from the knowledge of God

Assuredly, he who keeps silence ought not to conceive of all these things as merely so many words, but must indeed see each one of them made real in himself every day. If he is not sitting in his cell in order to live in this way, what is the use of enclosing his body with walls? The intellect is immaterial and bodiless. When contained not by walls but by the divine Spirit, it is firmly established in its natural condition and converses

---

5   The latter part of this description—sweetness, joy, tranquility, etc.—comprise traditional criteria for discerning the genuine-ness of an experience of God, as opposed to a demonic delu-sion. Note also here the appeal to the "spiritual senses:" "see," "handle," "taste."

with God. The one who thus sits alone in his cell, what other thing ought he to do if he has not understood exactly what we have been talking about and has not put them into continous spiritual practice? For unless he knows how to work spiritually, he who is at once removed from the commandments and at leisure from bodily activity is clearly idle on both counts. If, then, idleness is an evil, the man who stays in this condition is truly sinning, since the one who is knowledgeable in spiritual work is not hindered by his solitude from the practice of God's commandments which are accomplished by the body. To the contrary, he is instead greatly helped with respect to them and does them the more easily. On the other hand, he who gives evidence of his art only in what occurs on the outside—I mean the pursuit of asceticism—if he should pause from it, then he is no longer able to do what is spiritual either. How? Because he is carrying the tools and raw material around in his hand, and it is as if he were without experience in the craft and, unable to put it into practice and perfect it, his work is thus shown up as weak and unfruitful. Let me provide you with some other examples in order for you to grasp clearly what I am trying to say.

How many people, would you say, were ready to weep like the prostitute, but did not like her receive forgiveness? How many climbed up Mt Tabor—and climb it even now—but did not see the transfigured Lord, not, certainly, because Jesus the Christ was not present there (He is present), but because they were not worthy to see His divinity? How many of the Jews entered the house where the Apostles were staying without any of them receiving the Comforter? How many search the Scriptures and are entirely ignorant of Him Who speaks in them? How many breathed their last in caves and mountain crags without becoming more worthy than the world, such that the world would not be worthy of them, but were themselves—O, Your judgments, Lord!—numbered with the world? How many have withdrawn into silence, and do so now, who do not know the meaning of the word itself, let alone have anything to say about the mystery which is in silence? For the knowledge of God is not given by the outward silence, as certain people mistakenly understand the saying: "Be still, and know that I am God" [Ps 46:10], but silence rather arises from the knowledge of God in him who does battle lawfully and well. Because, if we call stillness the abstention from works, and silence sloth, and prefer these things instead of the doing of the commandments, how shall we fulfill the law of Christ and the order of the Apostles, the first of which says: "Whatever you wish that men would do to you, do so to them" [Mt 7:12]; and again: "If I then, your Lord and Teacher, have washed your feet, you also ought to wash one another's feet" [Jn 13:14]; and again: "If anyone would be first, he must be last of all and servant of all" [Mk 9:35]; and the second of which: "If anyone will not work, let him not eat" [II Thess 3:10]; and elsewhere: "In all things I have shown you that by so toiling one must help the weak" [Acts 20:35]; and: "These hands ministered to my necessities, and to those who were with me" [Acts 20:34].

True Knowledge is the foundation of Apostolic work

For all the Apostles, and the God-bearing fathers who followed them, nowhere preferred silence to what is well-pleasing to God through works, but giving evidence of their faith through their fulfillment of the commandments they were made worthy of the love of God in knowledge and, as having struggled according to the law, and receiving as a prize of victory the love of God in knowledge, and as longing to be with him, they departed the stadium and the tumult of combat. And still now, those who struggle lawfully depart these things rejoicing in the fruits of their labors without care and unmingled with what is below and sorrowful. When they have delighted without satiation in such great good, however, and are certain that, according to the Apostle: "The sufferings of this present time are not worth comparing to the glory that is to be revealed to us" [Rom 8:18]; and that: "Each shall receive his wages according to his labor" [I Cor 3:8], they are not satisfied with their prior exploits, but set forth once more from their comfort and from such delight to their struggles, according to the saying of the Theologian: "From silence to speech, not for themselves yet also for themselves, but for the honor of God Whom they love and by Whom they are loved in return."[6] No longer do they give and receive blows, nor are they engaged with their foes as before, but are frightful to them by their mere appearance. For they have only to appear and their enemies turn to flight. Those who had been wounded by the latter they immediately bind up, anoint, and teach how they must go against such opponents, with what kinds of weapons and what sort of strategies.

Unless the man who keeps silence, and he who presides over others, and he who teaches others understand each one of these things, the one who thinks he is keeping silence is not doing so, but sits in ignorance and only his body is enclosed; nor is the man who presides truly so, but only thinks so, yet by walking a road he does not know, or better going entirely off the path, he leads those who follow him together with himself over a cliff of eternal fire; nor is the one who thinks he teaches a teacher of others, but is a liar and deceiver because he does not possess within himself the true wisdom, our Lord Jesus Christ. For people like this, what need is there to talk about binding and loosing?[7] Those who do possess the Comforter in themselves shudder while forgiving sins, lest they do something contrary to the will of Him Who is in them and Who

6   From Gregory Nazianzus, *In laudem Athanasii*, *PG* 3 5.1104B. The quotation does not, however, exactly match.
7   See the *Letter on Confession*, esp. ¶ 13-14, in Vol. III, forthcoming.

speaks through them. But who is so insane and so taken with audacity as to say or do works of the Spirit before having received the Comforter, or do what is God's without God's consent? Woe to those who dare such things on the dread day of judgement on which the Lord, the Judge Who can neither be bribed nor deceived, sits upon His fearful throne and judgement seat, rendering to each according to his deeds and lusts and words, to Whom is due all glory, honor and worship, together with the Father and the Spirit, now and ever, and unto ages of ages without end. Amen.

Index of Scriptural References

Index

Other Titles in the Popular Patristics Series from St Vladimir's Seminary Press: